HISTORY OF LIFE

Patrick Flannery

To My Loving Mother

No day or hour passes that you're not on my mind. You listened when I talked to you in the hospital before you fell into a deep sleep. I said to you I couldn't wish for a better mother, with all the love and care you shared and gave to me. One lonely Christmas when I was all alone, I felt my life had fallen apart and all the people I thought would ring to wish me a happy new year and didn't. The phone rang, and it was you, my mother wishing me a happy new year. We talked and cried, and you were always there for me. It was so hard to let you go, but you taught me that when you love someone, you let them go with love. The loss of my mother, my best friend.

With love always, your son Patrick Flannery

My Life

This my life shall never be repeated,
it's no song that you can sing again.
So one day, since fate cannot be cheated,
I shall also pass to death's domain.

But whatever else I do while living,
This I beg of life before I'm done …
let me savour water, scent, rough weather
see the night stars, greet the rising sun.

I'd like happiness to call and see me,
And the finest feelings freely give.
If it's true that death will not release me,
How shall I unlearn to think and live.

Patrick Flannery
1994

Foreword

It has been said of Patrick Flannery that if he could read and write he would indeed be a very dangerous man. His first book gives a very unique insight into a man who has always shown passion and zest for everything he has done in his life, in his business as well as his interactions with others around him. Patrick is a man who sees the best in people but never suffers fools either. He is someone who has made a huge contribution to many people's lives and has put his own personal life experiences to good use in supporting others. This book is his life story to date and reading it will certainly have an impact on readers far and wide. Without Patrick's contribution to helping people and his own inputs and support, particularly to developing AA in the West of Ireland, many a person's life would have taken a totally different and probably worse direction. This book portrays how he grew up, completing his formal education at the age of 11, the strong and positive influence of his mother, where and how he made a difference to Erris and the many obstacles he encountered and overcame along the way. He provides lessons to people of all walks of life. His story is not only touching but tough. Patrick has walked through life standing up and fighting for his values, in particular for republicanism and his core inner belief in a united Ireland in control of and shaping its own future and destiny. In addition, Patrick has always been an advocate of communities and has consistently fought for those same communities to take responsibility for themselves. His own life story is an example of this.

His relationship with alcohol as he describes in his first book, *'Don't give Up'* is probably now as much of an asset to him as it was a liability in the past. He can reach out to people, and today has a greater understanding of human beings resulting from the many, many events and adventures in his own life.

Patrick is still a young man and long may his life of experiences, adventures and good things continue. It is in itself a milestone in his life to publish this work and leave a legacy of advice, life's insights and experiences to others.

Gerard Mc Donnell

Back to My Teenage Years

Today is the 19th August 2005 and there is a big heritage day on in Belmullet. A day that the local people come with their stalls and sell their goods on the streets. It's absolutely beautiful, great sunshine today in Belmullet. There are people from all over the world here, people that came back on holidays and are still here visiting around Belmullet. It's a day like the 15th August again this year, 2005, and there is one of the biggest crowds that was ever seen. It's a traditional day as well, going back for hundreds of years, where people come to town and still keep the tradition up. On the 15th August there is live music on the streets.

When we were growing up as kids in Porturlin, we were always looking forward to the 15th August. It was a big thing for us all to come into Belmullet and we would spend the day in the town. Then as we were growing older, that night after the fair in the town, we would go out dancing to 'Palm Court' and would enjoy a great night of dancing. We used to look forward to it from year to year and it was one marvellous day, and still the tradition continues today. A lot of people are dressed up today in the old fashioned way and carrying on the tradition. It's great to see the people out enjoying themselves.

A lot of time in my life I would be around people that don't want to enjoy themselves, and when you are around people like that, they will pull you down. People in my life that I have seen getting up in the morning, always in bad humour, always complaining about something and I do not really want to be around them. They are not my type of people. When it is a genuine or serious concern, I will understand then that they have something to complain about. But I realise that there are people who go out of their way to find something to complain about. Earlier today I was listening to some of that complaining, and I just got dressed and left. I went into Belmullet to enjoy myself and that's where I was today. I always do, it's a special day, meeting people that are out on the town, and it's absolutely great to be able to do that, to have the health to do that. It's great to be able to get up in the morning and be healthy besides getting up in the morning complaining. I just cannot live around people like that who are moaning and groaning. I love positive people, people who are smiling and happy, it makes going through life a lot easier compared to people who don't do that.

When we were kids, the 15th of August was always a big day. We looked so forward to it. Our fathers would be fishing for the salmon for seven weeks and seven days a week. On the 12th of August they would make up the money that they had earned over those seven weeks, and it would be divided up among the crew and the skipper. Our fathers would give us so much money for the 15th August so that we could spend it and enjoy it on that day. I see it, even to this day, the kids spending their money on the 15th August at the fair. It's a great day, it's a family day and you are meeting people who are home on holidays. If you meet a fisherman you're talking about fishing, if you meet a farmer you're talking about farming and builders and so on. There is a great buzz in Erris.

Indeed there was always a buzz in Erris, but with the last ten years there is a massive buzz, with the new 72-bedroom hotel, so many restaurants in the town now. The whole town has completely changed, all new buildings, and it's great to see it. There are houses going up everywhere. People are thinking positively and it's great. They are moving forward and have better houses and homes now.

It's only with the last fifteen years in this country that people have started borrowing money from the banks and the banks have started lending money. When I was growing up, as a kid or even a teenager, there was no such thing as borrowing money from them. I believe that we didn't have to borrow money because we were fishing. Once we left the cradle, from eleven years old, I was fishing and so were my brothers. We were involved in making money from the sea. We wouldn't dream of borrowing money and indeed nobody would borrow money at that time. Whatever you had was your own. Like my father and mother, they didn't have a mortgage on their house, the little house that we had. Everybody was the same, what they had was their own. But today there are big houses with people borrowing up to one hundred per cent for their homes. People today are taking more chances; it's different times, totally different. The banks are encouraging people to borrow now; they are giving people cards now for the hole in the wall and the money will come out through the wall. It's all to tempt people, tempting students to borrow money as well. I think the banks are gangsters really; they are encouraging people to borrow more and more money. There is nothing wrong with borrowing money as long as you have a solid footing, that whatever you are borrowing for is fairly solid and you don't have to work all the hours God ever gives to pay back these banks. It's changed times and there are definitely better homes now. But it's a different way of life. There is more of a rush on this country today and the people than there was when we were growing up, and in my father and mother's time. But back then, we were looking forward to the 12th August and the money being made up. It would be divided up at my mother and father's house, on the table and all the kids would be around the table. We would all get money for the 15th August to have a good day out and to buy whatever we wanted.

My mother would make food for my father and the crew and there would also be drink there for the crew, it was a celebration for the end of the salmon season and the money made. I remember the table being full with the money, an awful lot of money. It was nice to see it. And we were all a big happy family - that's the way that we were brought up. Whatever my father or mother earned would be all shared out and whatever they were thinking about, they would always share it with all the family. My father would always hand over the fishing money to my mother to buy the food for all of us and to look after us for the rest of the year. It was a nice experience to have this money on the 15th August to buy your clothes in Seamus Cafferkey's, clothes that would take you through the year. We looked so forward then to going out to 'Palm Court'. I loved going out there, dancing, I loved all the dance halls around Glenamoy, there was four nights that you could go out dancing if you wanted to.

We went dancing young too because we were out earning money at a young age, all we cared about was having enough money to get into the dance halls. We enjoyed the night, there was no such thing as drinking out in the few cars that were around at that time. Then the next night we would talk about the dance from the night before, people were happy then.

I used to get all the dances! The girls used to be mad for me to dance with them. I learned to dance when I was about twelve years old. My sisters taught me to jive, and we used to be practising the jiving in the house and waltzing as well. I turned out to be a fairly good jiver so I used to get all the dances. I went into the dance hall to dance, I would be out on the floor dancing. I wouldn't be standing around looking at people or be afraid to dance. I would be out for every jive and every waltz and I used to enjoy it to the last. I remember I had a habit when I was a young fella, I'd always say to a girl "Keep the last dance for me" and sometimes I might go back and dance with them and most times I wouldn't! But there was a time anyway, after a girl I was dating, my teenage love, that I would go to Palm Court that she would hold the dance for me. We'd be dancing and talking and chatting all night and then we'd go up to the mineral bar and have a minerals and I remember there was Club Milk's out. That's the sort of relationship that we had and then we'd meet every Sunday night. We became good friends as well, she loved jiving and was a good jiver and I used to enjoy her company and we'd chat about everything - about our families and all that.

Then when I would come home from the dance I would tell my mother about who I was with, but I used to tell her not to tell anyone else. And my mother used to say that she wouldn't tell anyone else but I realise that she used to tell all of the family! One night anyway, I thought that she was going with somebody else behind my back, and there was a dance on in Aughoose, and she wanted to go to it. There used to be a dance in Aughoose on Wednesday nights, and I told her that I wasn't going. I went home and the weekend came and the following Wednesday came and it was time for the dance in Aughoose again and I remember going to the dance that night, thinking that she would be there. When I got to the dance her two friends, that knew me well, were there and they saw me out dancing and enjoying myself for the night. They came up to me and they were angry because they said that she wouldn't go to the dance because she thought that I wouldn't be there. I felt like a real prick to have done that to her. She was a genuine young girl but my mind was thinking that she might have been going out with somebody else but she wasn't. But anyway her two friends reared up on me and I begged them not to tell her. At the end of the dance, I walked the last girl that I was dancing with to the car and the two friends saw me and they thought that I was with this girl, but I wasn't. But then the next night we went back to Palm Court in the car, a gang of us, and I had a date on with her again. I wouldn't dance with her until three or four dances from the end of the night, I had three dates for that night, I had told them to save the last dance for me. When the last dance came the three women must have got talking about 'Patrick' and saving the last dance for me but there was only one girl that I wanted to go dancing with. When I asked her to dance she said that she wouldn't dance with me. She said that I went to the dance in Aughoose without her and she was mad. But anyway we made up again after that and became friends again. It's a long story after that.

She went to England and I went to Scotland and we were supposed to meet up again in August but we never met up. Years went by and we never met each other but I always wondered what happened to her. When I did eventually meet up with her, it was when her father was dying and that was the first time that I had seen her in years. I was in the hospital in Belmullet, with my daughter Maria, visiting my father in law and there was a man in the next bed. Two ladies walked in to visit him and, after all those years that I never seen her, there was Theresa and her sister visiting their father. I walked out and as I passed her she said "Patrick" and we talked. We talked about both our lives all the way back to when were teenagers. I told her about my life as a fisherman and publican. I also told her that I started drinking when I was twenty and she couldn't believe it because in my young days she said "you always hated drink". I told her that today I counsel people to help them stop drinking. Then her father died and I went to the funeral. She could talk to me about anything, she knew that even when we were younger that we could talk and share anything that was in our lives - and we did. I always talked to her about my father and my mother. I hated drink at that time - I wouldn't look at drink. All I wanted was to go to the dances and enjoy myself.

Years went by and I married and I had kids and she did as well. The only relationship that we had was when we met up and she shared her life with me. She talked to me for the first time about years ago in Palm Court. She is back in Manchester nursing, which is what she always wanted to do, even when she was young, she would tell me that she wanted to be nursing. And of course I wanted to be a fisherman and we used to share our dreams like that. But that was our life as teenager, it was all innocent. There was no harm in it and there was no love making or sex or that kind of thing going on, it was just that you would be going out to the dance with a girl, you wouldn't be going out with them for sex. You went out to enjoy yourself - the women and the men. The few that did go out to have sex, well they got their girlfriends pregnant and they ended up marrying them or the girls ended up marrying them. That was the way it was. But it was good times, I have good memories of going out dancing around Erris and enjoying myself. We went out to enjoy ourselves - we didn't go out to row or fight and even in them times you would see a lot of fighting. But the Porturlin lads wouldn't be into that type of thing - we used to work hard at the sea and then our reward was going out dancing with all the young girls and with our friends. We had good friends, I had a lot of good girl friends, as friends. We used to meet up in Palm Court and sit around the table with our 'Coke' or 'Orange' - them were the only two drinks that were available. Unlike today, there are all types of drinks going.

I'd come home and share the night with my mother and she would be delighted to hear all about it. She would love to hear who I had met at the dance, the girlfriend I had, and who I danced with, and she would know the mother and the father of these people and she would be delighted with me telling her all this. I shared everything with my mother in my young days. It was very easy to talk to my mother and I wouldn't talk to her until the rest of the family were all gone out of the house. She was a good, warm woman. I remember her telling me to always treat women the way that you would treat your mother, always show respect to women. And we did and they treated us with respect too.

There were thirteen in my family - my mother and father reared us to always look out for each other, and even our friends - boys or girls - we always looked out for each other. We made sure that we always looked out for each other, there was a great bond there as a family, as there was with the other families in Porturlin too. We made sure that everyone was ok.

Tom & Eileen on their wedding day, my father and mother, good parents who reared 13 of us.

The night before the wedding Tom was fishing for salmon, the morning of the wedding he came in from fishing and met JJ O'Donnell his best man who brought him in a pickup truck to Bangor where they got married.

Catherine & Tom Flannery, my Grandparents

Margaret McDonnell Moran

Photographs of my grandmother, Margaret McDonnell Moran

Margaret
McDonnell
Moran

Mary
Moran
Bennett

Margaret

Margaret

Margaret

Caroline
Bennett

More photographs of my grandmother, Margaret McDonnell Moran, along with Mary Moran Bennett and Caroline Bennett.

13 brothers and sisters all grew up together in Porturlin

Family members included in the 1911 Census

(Source: The National Archives of Ireland)

The National Archives of Ireland

GENEALOGY

- Home
- Search Census
- Early 20th century Ireland
- Browse Census
- How to Search

- Census Years
- 1911
- Mayo
- Muingnabo
- Porturlin
- Residents of a house

1911 Census

Residents of a house 10 in Porturlin (Muingnabo, Mayo)

☐ Show all information

Surname	Forename	Age	Sex	Relation to head	Religion	Birthplace	Occupation	Literacy	Irish Language	Marital Status	Specified Illnesses	Years Married	Children Born	Children Living
McDonnell	James	69	Male	Head of Family	Roman Catholic	Mayo	Farmer	Read and write	Irish and English	Married	-	-	-	-
McDonnell	Kate	52	Female	Wife	Roman Catholic	Mayo	-	Read	Irish and English	Married	-	33	9	9
McDonnell	Pat	30	Male	Son	Roman Catholic	Mayo	-	Read and write	Irish and English	Single	-	-	-	-
McDonnell	Martin	26	Male	Son	Roman Catholic	Mayo	-	Read and write	Irish and English	Single	-	-	-	-
McDonnell	Annie	22	Female	Daughter	Roman Catholic	Mayo	Lace Making	Read and write	Irish and English	Single	-	-	-	-
McDonnell	Mary	19	Female	Daughter	Roman Catholic	Mayo	Lace Making	Read and write	Irish and English	Single	-	-	-	-
McDonnell	Jon	17	Male	Son	Roman Catholic	Mayo	Scholar	Read and write	Irish and English	Single	-	-	-	-
McDonnell	James	16	Male	Son	Roman Catholic	Mayo	Scholar	Read and write	Irish and English	Single	-	-	-	-
McDonnell	Magie	14	Female	Daughter	Roman Catholic	Mayo	Scholar	Read and write	Irish and English	Single	-	-	-	-
McDonnell	Katie	6	Female	Daughter	Roman Catholic	Mayo	Scholar	Read	Irish and English	Single	-	-	-	-
McDonnell	John	5	Male	Son	Roman Catholic	Mayo	Scholar	Cannot read	-	Single	-	-	-	-

My grandmother (handwritten, next to McDonnell Magie row)

Report any error in transcription

View census images

Household Return (Form A)
Additional Pages: 2

CENSUS OF IRELAND, 1911.

Form N.—Enumerator's Abstract for a Townland or Street.

County _Mayo [R]_   Superintendent's Registrar's Division _Mayo [Lalt?]_   Union or Poor Law Union _Belmullet_   District Electoral Division _Muingna Co._   Townland or Street _[Tortorlee]_

Constabulary District _Belmullet_   Sub-District _Rossport_   Barony _Erris_   Parish _Kilcommon_

ABSTRACT showing the Number of Dwelling-houses, Families, and Persons in the above-named Townland or Street, also the Religious Profession (so far as ascertained), of the People enumerated by _[Jno. Wyllies]_

Note.—This Abstract should be carefully filled by the Enumerator, and attached in front of his File of the several Forms for the persons enumerated in the Townland or Street to which it relates.

Signed: J. B. DOUGHERTY, (Under-Secretary.)
  WILLIAM J. THOMPSON, (Registrar-General.) (Commissioners.)
  EDWARD O'FARRELL,
  DANIEL B. BUTLER.

No.	Inhabited	Uninhabited	Building	Families in each House	Males	Females	Total Number of Persons	Roman Catholics		Church of Ireland		Others (So far)																
								Males	Females																		
1	1			1	6	4	10	6	4																		
2	1			1	2	4	6	2	4																		
3	1			1	3	5	8	3	5																		
4	1			1	1	1	2	1	1																		
5	1			1	3	6	9	3	6																		
6	1			1	3	2	5	3	2																		
7	1			1	3	3	6	3	3																		
8	1			1	1	4	5	1	4																		
9	1			1	6	5	11	6	5																		
10	1			1	3	3	6	3	3																		
11 foral	11			11	35	38	73	35	38																		

Form N.—Enumerator's Abstract for a Townland or Street—continued.

No.	Inhabited	Uninhabited	Building	Families in each House	Males	Females	Total Number of Persons	Roman Catholics																			
								Males	Females																		
Brought ovr	11			11	35	38	73	35	38																		
12	4			1	3	3	6	3	3																		
13	1			1	1	2	3	1	2																		
14	1			1	3	0	3	3	0																		
15	1			1	1	5	6	1	5																		
16	1			1	3	0	3	3	0																		
17	1			1	4	5	9	4	5																		
18	1			1	4	5	9	4	5																		
19	1			1	2	1	3	2	1																		
20	1			1	4	2	6	4	3																		
21							5																				
Total	47		22	63	71	139	67	74																			

Mark J Fallon Signature of Enumerator

Dated this _7th_ day of _May_, 1911.

FORM B. 1.—HOUSE AND BUILDING RETURN.

FORM B. 1.—HOUSE AND BUILDING RETURN—continued.

Approved,
J. B. DOUGHERTY,
Dublin Castle,
15th December, 1910.

WILLIAM J. THOMPSON,
Registrar-General,
EDWARD O'FARRELL,
DANIEL S. DOYLE,

I hereby Certify, as required by the Act to Edw. VII and 1 Geo. V., cap. 11, sec. 6 (1) that the foregoing Return is correct, according to the best of my knowledge and belief.

Second Page. Superintendent Registrar's District of _Belmullet_

66

19__ Marriage solemnized at the Roman Catholic _Chapel_ of _Kilcommon Erris_ in the Registrar's District of _Knocknalower_
in the Union of _Belmullet_ in the County of _Mayo_

No. (1)	When Married (2)	Name and Surname (3)	Age (4)	Condition (5)	Rank or Profession (6)	Residence at the Time of Marriage (7)	Father's Name and Surname (8)	Rank or Profession of Father (9)
48	6th February 1917	James O'Donnell	25	Bachelor	Farmer	Cumlet	James O'Donnell	Farmer
		Mary McCadas	30	Spinster	—	Goltbock	John McCadas	Farmer

Married in the Roman Catholic _Chapel_ of _Kilcommon Erris_ according to the Rites and Ceremonies of the Roman Catholic Church by me, _A. Tinlin PP_

This Marriage was solemnized between us, { James O'Donnell / Mary McCadas } in the Presence of us, { Anthony O'Donnell, Patrick A. Tinlin }

Marriage No. 48. Registered by me, this 9th day of July 1917.

---

19 17 Marriage solemnized at the Roman Catholic _Chapel_ of _Kilcommon Erris_ in the Registrar's District of _Knocknalower_
in the Union of _Belmullet_ in the County of _Mayo_

No. (1)	When Married (2)	Name and Surname (3)	Age (4)	Condition (5)	Rank or Profession (6)	Residence at the Time of Marriage (7)	Father's Name and Surname (8)	Rank or Profession of Father (9)
49	2nd March 1917	John Flannery	28	Bachelor	Farmer	Portaclay	James Flannery	Farmer
		Mary McDonnell	25	Spinster	—	Portaclay	James McDonnell	Farmer

Married in the Roman Catholic _Church_ of _Kilcommon Erris_ according to the Rites and Ceremonies of the Roman Catholic Church by me, _A. Tinlin PP_

This Marriage was solemnized between us, { John Flannery / Mary McDonnell } in the Presence of us, { Michael Flannery, Mary J. Flannery, Patrick A. Tinlin PP }

Marriage No. 49. Registered by me, this 9th day of July 1917.

---

19 17 Marriage solemnized at the Roman Catholic _Church_ of _Kilcommon Erris_ in the Registrar's District of _Knocknalower_
in the Union of _Belmullet_ in the County of _Mayo_

No. (1)	When Married (2)	Name and Surname (3)	Age (4)	Condition (5)	Rank or Profession (6)	Residence at the Time of Marriage (7)	Father's Name and Surname (8)	Rank or Profession of Father (9)
50	6th March 1917	Charles O'Donnell	30	Bachelor	Farmer	Aughoose	Charles O'Donnell (deceased)	Farmer
		Maggie Norne	30	Spinster	—	Knocknalower	Pat Norne	Farmer

Married in the Roman Catholic _Church_ of _Kilcommon Erris_ according to the Rites and Ceremonies of the Roman Catholic Church by me, _Thomas Browne CC_

This Marriage was solemnized between us, { Charles O'Donnell / Maggie Norne } in the Presence of us, { Martin O'Donnell, James McGuire }

Marriage No. 50. Registered by me, this 9th day of July 1917.

---

19 17 Marriage solemnized at the Roman Catholic _Church_ of _Kilcommon Erris_ in the Registrar's District of _Knocknalower_
in the Union of _Belmullet_ in the County of _Mayo_

No. (1)	When Married (2)	Name and Surname (3)	Age (4)	Condition (5)	Rank or Profession (6)	Residence at the Time of Marriage (7)	Father's Name and Surname (8)	Rank or Profession of Father (9)
51	6th March 1917	Pat McHale	30	Bachelor	Farmer	Belding	Pat McHale	Farmer
		Anne McDonnell	28	Spinster	—	Glenamoy	John McDonnell	Farmer

Married in the Roman Catholic _Church_ of _Kilcommon Erris_ according to the Rites and Ceremonies of the Roman Catholic Church by me, _Thomas Browne CC_

This Marriage was solemnized between us, { Patrick McHale / Anne McDonnell } in the Presence of us, { Pat McDonnell, John McDonnell }

Marriage No. 51. Registered by me, this 9th day of July 1917.

I, _____, Registrar of Marriages, in the District of _Knocknalower_ in the Union of _Belmullet_ in the County of _Mayo_, do hereby Certify, That this is a true copy of the Registrar's Book of Marriages within the said District from the Entry of the Marriage of _James O'Donnell_ and _Mary McCadas_ Number 48, to the Entry of the Marriage of _Pat McHale_ and _Anne McDonnell_ Number 51.

Witness my hand, this 20th day of October 1917. _____ Registrar.

I have examined the above, and have compared it with the said original Registrar's Book, and hereby certify that it is a true copy. Witness my hand this 23rd day of Oct 1917. _J. O'Reilly_ Superintendent Registrar.

(handwritten note in left margin)
Mar 2, 1917
Wedding
→
John Flannery and Mary McDonnell

- 15 -

Superintendent Registrar's District of _Knockbrack_

05287188

34

19 2_. Marriage solemnized at the Roman Catholic _Church_ at _Bonboy_ **in the Registrar's District of** _Knockbrack_
in the Union of _Belmullet_ **in the County of** _Mayo_

When Married. (1)	Name and Surname. (2)	Age. (3)	Condition. (4)	Rank or Profession. (5)	Residence at the Time of Marriage. (6)	Father's Name and Surname. (7)	Rank or Profession of Father. (8)	
6th Sept 1920	John Coyle	aged	Buchlr	Farmer	Doohoma	John Coyle	Farmer	Marriage No. 78
	Mary McGannon	aged	Spinstr	Farmer	Roosfad S.	Anthony McGannon	Farmer	Registered by me, this 6th day of July 1928.

Married in the Roman Catholic _Church_ at _Bonboy_ according to the Rites and Ceremonies of the Roman Catholic Church by me, _M. Hannely, CC._

This Marriage was solemnized between us, { John Coyle / Mary x McGannon } in the Presence of us, { Patrick Barrett / James McGannon }

W. H. Smith, Registrar, dep.

19 25. Marriage solemnized at the Roman Catholic _Church_ at _Bonboy_ **in the Registrar's District of** _Knockbrack_
in the Union of _Belmullet_ **in the County of** _Mayo_

When Married. (1)	Name and Surname. (2)	Age. (3)	Condition. (4)	Rank or Profession. (5)	Residence at the Time of Marriage. (6)	Father's Name and Surname. (7)	Rank or Profession of Father. (8)	
4th February 1925	Thomas Cormack	aged	Buchlr Farmer	Farmer	Roosfad N.	John Cormack	Farmer	Marriage No. 79
	Bridget Moran	aged	Spinstr	Farmer	Bonboy	Pat Moran	Farmer	Registered by me, this 6th day of July 1928.

Married in the Roman Catholic _Church_ at _Bonboy_ according to the Rites and Ceremonies of the Roman Catholic Church by me, _M. Hannely, CC._

This Marriage was solemnized between us, { Thomas Cormack / Bridget x Moran } in the Presence of us, { Patrick McGrath Wm M. Hannely CC / Mary Boylan }

W. H. Smith, Registrar, dep.

19 26. Marriage solemnized at the Roman Catholic _Church_ at _Bonboy_ **in the Registrar's District of** _Knockbrack_
in the Union of _Belmullet_ **in the County of** _Mayo_

When Married. (1)	Name and Surname. (2)	Age. (3)	Condition. (4)	Rank or Profession. (5)	Residence at the Time of Marriage. (6)	Father's Name and Surname. (7)	Rank or Profession of Father. (8)	
4th January 1926	Thomas Hanaty	49	Widower	Farmer	Shraigh	Thomas Hanaty	Farmer	Marriage No. 76
	Catherine Foyle	36	Spinstr	—	Rathlea	Pat Foyle	Farmer	Registered by me, this 6th day of July 1928.

Married in the Roman Catholic _Church_ at _Bonboy_ according to the Rites and Ceremonies of the Roman Catholic Church by me, _Michael J. Murphy, CC._

This Marriage was solemnized between us, { Thomas x Hanaty / Catherine Foyle } in the Presence of us, { Patrick McDonnellMaggie McDonnell }

W. H. Smith, Registrar, dep.

19 . Marriage solemnized at the Roman Catholic at **in the Registrar's District of**
in the Union of **in the County of**

When Married. (1)	Name and Surname. (2)	Age. (3)	Condition. (4)	Rank or Profession. (5)	Residence at the Time of Marriage. (6)	Father's Name and Surname. (7)	Rank or Profession of Father. (8)	
								Marriage No.
								Registered by me, this day of 19

Married in the Roman Catholic of according to the Rites and Ceremonies of the Roman Catholic Church by me,

This Marriage was solemnized between us, { } in the Presence of us, { }

Registrar.

W. H. Smith Registrar of Marriages, in the District of _Knockbrack_ in the
Union of _Belmullet_ in the County of _Mayo_ do hereby Certify, That this is a true copy of the Registrar's Book of Marriage within
the said District from the Entry of the Marriage of _John Coyle_ and _Mary McGannon_ Number 78 to the Entry of the Marriage
of _Thomas Hanaty_ and _Catherine Foyle_ Number 79 Witness my hand, this 5th day of October 1928. _W. H. Smith dep._ Registrar.
I have examined the above, and compared it with the said original Registrar's Book, and hereby certify that it is a true copy.
Witness my hand this 20th day of October 1928. _W. Henry SR_ Superintendent Registrar.

- 16 -

Second Page.

[Please note that all Copies made on this Page should be certified at foot.]

01538229

Superintendent Registrar's District _Belmullet_   Registrar's District _Knocknalower_

BIRTHS Registered in the District of _Knocknalower_ in the Union of _Belmullet_

in the County of _Mayo_

No. (1)	Date and Place of Birth (2)	Name (if any) (3)	Sex (4)	Name and Surname and Dwelling-place of Father (5)	Name and Surname and Maiden Surname of Mother (6)	Rank or Profession of Father (7)	Signature, Qualification, and Residence of Informant (8)	When Registered (9)	Signature of Registrar (10)	Baptismal Name if added after registration (11)
439	1917 May _Ballyglass_ Stonefield	Mary Kate	F	Michael Connolly Stonefield	Kate Connolly formerly Gaven	Farmer	Michael Connolly mark Father Stonefield	July 1917	E.H. Fitzgerald Registrar	
440	July _second_ Aglone	Jane	F	John O'Donnell Aglone	Mary O'Donnell formerly King	Farmer	John O'Donnell Father Aglone	July 1917	E.H. Fitzgerald Registrar	
441	June _Ballyglass_ Gortmellia	Michael	M	Anthony Doherty Gortmellia	Kate Doherty formerly McHale	Farmer	Anthony Doherty mark Father Gortmellia	July 1917	E.H. Fitzgerald Registrar	
442	1917 June _second_ Glengad	Anne	F	Martin McGrath Glengad	formerly				Registrar	
443	June _Ballyglass_ Conboy	Edward	M	Michael Murray Conboy	Margaret Murray formerly Gallagle	Farmer	Michael Murray mark Father Conboy	July 1917	E.H. Fitzgerald Registrar	
444	July _Ballyglass_ Rossport	Bridget Agnes	F	Michael McGarry Rossport	Bridget McGarry formerly Gerraty	Farmer	Michael McGarry Father Rossport	July 1917	E.H. Fitzgerald Registrar	
445	1917 July _fourth_ Shadoggle	Kate	F	James Doherty Shadoggle	Kate Doherty formerly Toole	Farmer	James Doherty Father Shadoggle	July 1917	E.H. Fitzgerald Registrar	
446	July _fourteenth_ Muinginate	Mary	F	Michael Gaven Muinginate	Mary Gaven formerly Flannery	Farmer	Michael Gaven Father Muinginate	July 1917	E.H. Fitzgerald Registrar	
447	1917 July _thirteenth_ Porturlin	Kate	F	John Flannery Porturlin	Mary Flannery formerly O'Donnell	Farmer	John Flannery Father Porturlin	July 1917	E.H. Fitzgerald Registrar	
448	1917 July _fourteenth_ Aglone	Anthony	M	Martin Conway Aglone	Celia Conway formerly McDonnell	Farmer	Martin Conway Father Aglone	July 1917	E.H. Fitzgerald Registrar	

Birth of Daughter
July 13, 1917

I, E.H. Fitzgerald Dtr. Registrar of Births and Deaths in the District of _Knocknalower_ in the Union of _Belmullet_ in the County of _Mayo_ do hereby certify, that this is a true copy of the Registrar's Book of Births within the said District, from the Entry of the Birth of _Mary Kate Connolly_ in the Entry of the Birth of _Anthony Conway_ No. _448_ Witness my hand, this _20th_ day of _Octr 19_   E.H. Fitzgerald Dtr. Registrar.

I have examined the above, and compared it with the said original Registrar's Book, and hereby certify that it is a true Copy. Witness my hand, this _23rd_ day _Octr 19_ J. O'Reilly Superintendent Registrar.

Death of infant
Son
Feb 5,
1922

Superintendent Registrar's District _Balmaclel_   Registrar's District _Knockbain_

20__   DEATHS Registered in the District of _Knockbain_   in the Union of _Balmaclel_   45

in the County of _Mayo_

No. (1)	Date and Place of Death (2)	Name and Surname (3)	Sex (4)	Condition (5)	Age last Birthday (6)	Rank, Profession, or Occupation (7)	Certified Cause of Death and Duration of Illness (8)	Signature, Qualification, and Residence of Informant (9)	When Registered (10)	Signature of Registrar (11)
465	19.22 Tenney 5th Nav. year	John Tenney	M	Bachelor	1 mth	Farmer's son	Senile Debil. 1 month no medical attendant	John and Tenney Letts Tenena year year	April 10th 1922	H. ... Jield Rd. Registrar
466	19.22	Jane Douglas	M	Married	60 year	Farmer	Chronic Bright 4 years No medical attendant	Jane Douglas do present at death Knockbain	April 10th 1922	H. ... Jield Rd. Registrar
467	19.22		?	Widow	70 year					

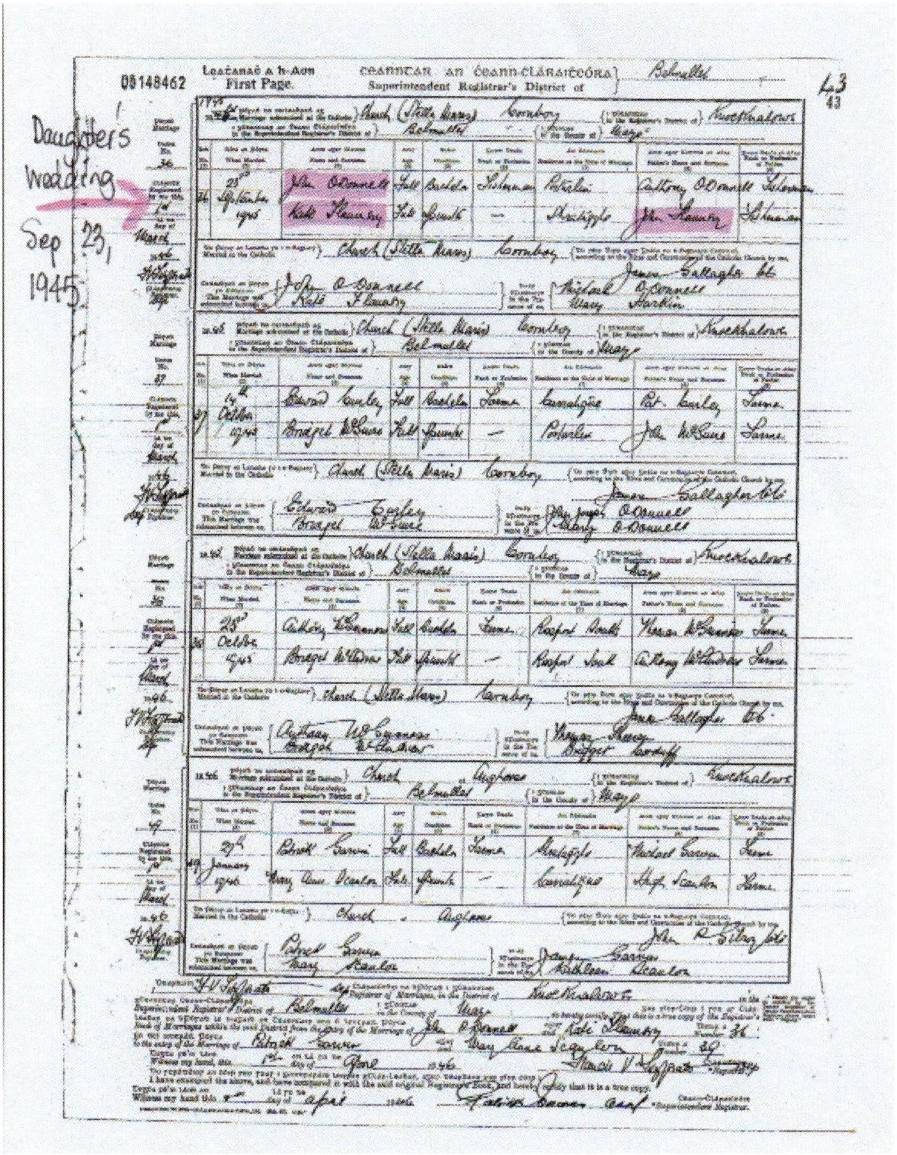

OB148462

Leaṫanaċ a h-Aon
First Page

CeAnntAr An ĊeAnn-ĊláráiṫeórA
Superintendent Registrar's District of   Belmullet

43
/43

1945

Church (Stella Maris)   Corraboy | I. Mórainn in the Registrar's District of   Knockalough
y Ġleannṫa an Ċeann Ċláráiṫeóra in the Superintendent Registrar's District of   Belmullet | in the County of   Mayo

No. 36	When Married	Name and Surname	Age	Condition	Rank or Profession	Residence at the Time of Marriage	Father's Name and Surname	Rank or Profession of Father
	25 September 1945	John O'Donnell	Full	Bachelor	Fisherman	Portacloy	Anthony O'Donnell	Fisherman
		Kate Flannery	Full	Spinster	—	Portacloy	Jn. Flannery	Fisherman

Married in the Catholic   Church (Stella Maris)   Corraboy
This Marriage   John   O'Donnell | in the Presence   Michael O'Donnell
solemnized between us   Kate   Flannery | of us   Mary Harkin | witnesses { James Gallagher C.C.

(remaining register entries below, largely illegible)

1946   Church (Stella Maris)   Corraboy   Knockalough   Mayo
Belmullet

| No. 37 | 6 October 1945 | Edward Cawley | Full | Bachelor | Farmer | Carnalughe | Pat. Cawley | Farmer |
| | | Bridget McGuire | Full | Spinster | — | Porturlin | John McGuire | Farmer |

Church (Stella Maris)   Corraboy
Edward Cawley   Bridget McGuire   James Gallagher C.C.
John Joyce O'Donnell   Mary O'Donnell

1946   Church (Stella Maris)   Corraboy   Knockalough   Mayo
Belmullet

| No. 38 | 25 October 1945 | Anthony McGuane | Full | Bachelor | Farmer | Rosport Nault | Thomas McGuane | Farmer |
| | | Bridget Williams | Full | Spinster | — | Rosport Nault | Anthony Williams | Farmer |

Church (Stella Maris)   Corraboy
Anthony McGuane   Bridget Williams   James Gallagher C.C.
Thomas Ruane   Bridget Cardiff

1946   Church of Aughoose   Knockalough   Mayo
Belmullet

| No. 4 | 29 January 1946 | Patrick Gavin | Full | Bachelor | Farmer | Gralagh | Michael Gavin | Farmer |
| | | Mary Anne Scanlon | Full | Spinster | — | Carnalughe | Stephen Scanlon | Farmer |

Church of Aughoose
Patrick Gavin   Mary Scanlon   James Gavin   Kathleen Scanlon

(certification section, illegible)

34

19 24. Marriage solemnized at the Roman Catholic *Church* at *Cornboy* in the Registrar's District of *Knockalough*
in the Union of *Belmullet* in the County of *Mayo*

No. (1)	When Married (2)	Name and Surname (3)	Age (4)	Condition (5)	Rank or Profession (6)	Residence at the Time of Marriage (7)	Father's Name and Surname (8)	Rank or Profession of Father (9)	
75	6th April 1924	John *Coyle*	aged	Bachelor	Farmer	*Sraphard*	*Owen Coyle*	Farmer	Marriage No. 78 Registered by me, this 6th day of July 1928 *H McDonald* Registrar, Asp.
		Mary *McGannon*	aged	Spinster	Farmer	*Roophal S.*	Anthony *McGannon*	Farmer	

Married in the Roman Catholic *Church* at *Cornboy* according to the Rites and Ceremonies of the Roman Catholic Church by me, *M. Mannelly CC*
This Marriage was solemnized between us, John *Coyle*, Mary *McGannon* in the Presence of us, *Patrick Hewitt*, Anne *McGannon*
Witness to marriage M. Mannelly CC

19 25. Marriage solemnized at the Roman Catholic *Church* at *Cornboy* in the Registrar's District of *Knockalough*
in the Union of *Belmullet* in the County of *Mayo*

No. (1)	When Married (2)	Name and Surname (3)	Age (4)	Condition (5)	Rank or Profession (6)	Residence at the Time of Marriage (7)	Father's Name and Surname (8)	Rank or Profession of Father (9)	
76	12th February 1925	Thomas *Cornwall*	aged	Bachelor Farmer	Farmer	*Roophal N.*	John *Cornwall*	Farmer	Marriage No. 79 Registered by me, this 6th day of July 1928 *H McDonald* Registrar, Asp.
		Bridget *Moran*	aged	Spinster	Farmer	*Cornboy*	Pat *Moran*	Farmer	

Married in the Roman Catholic *Church* at *Cornboy* according to the Rites and Ceremonies of the Roman Catholic Church by me, *M. Mannelly CC*
Witness M. Mannelly CC
This Marriage was solemnized between us, Thomas *Cornwall*, Bridget *Moran* in the Presence of us, *Peter McGrath*, Mary *Brogan*
Witness M. Mannelly CC

19 26. Marriage solemnized at the Roman Catholic *Church* at *Cornboy* in the Registrar's District of *Knockalough*
in the Union of *Belmullet* in the County of *Mayo*

No. (1)	When Married (2)	Name and Surname (3)	Age (4)	Condition (5)	Rank or Profession (6)	Residence at the Time of Marriage (7)	Father's Name and Surname (8)	Rank or Profession of Father (9)	
77	4th January 1926	Thomas *Heaney*	47	Widower	Farmer	*Shanaggin*	Thomas *Heaney*	Farmer	Marriage No. 80 Registered by me, this 6th day of July 1928 *H McDonald* Registrar, Asp.
		Catherine *Ogle*	36	Spinster	—	*Portacloi*	Pat *Ogle*	Farmer	

Married in the Roman Catholic *Church* at *Cornboy* according to the Rites and Ceremonies of the Roman Catholic Church by me, *Michael J. Murphy CC*
Witness M. J. Murphy CC
This Marriage was solemnized between us, Thomas *Heaney*, Catherine *Ogle* in the Presence of us, *Patrick O'Donnell*, *Maggie McCormack*

19__. Marriage solemnized at the Roman Catholic _____ at _____ in the Registrar's District of _____
in the Union of _____ in the County of _____

No. (1)	When Married (2)	Name and Surname (3)	Age (4)	Condition (5)	Rank or Profession (6)	Residence at the Time of Marriage (7)	Father's Name and Surname (8)	Rank or Profession of Father (9)	
									Marriage No. Registered by me, this day of 19__ Registrar.

Married in the Roman Catholic _____ of _____ according to the Rites and Ceremonies of the Roman Catholic Church by me, _____
This Marriage was solemnized between us, _____ in the Presence of us, _____

I, *H McDonald* Registrar of Marriages, in the District of *Knockalough*, in the Union of *Belmullet* in the County of *Mayo* do hereby Certify, That this is a true copy of the Registrar's Book of Marriages within the said District from the Entry of the Marriage of *John Coyle* and *Mary McGannon* Number 78 to the Entry of the Marriage of *Thomas Heaney* and *Catherine Ogle* Number 80 *Francis P. Synod* Asp. * Registrar.
Witness my hand, this 5th day of *July* 1928

I have examined the above, and have compared it with the said original Registrar's Book, and hereby certify that it is a true copy.
Witness my hand this 20th day of *October* 1928. *M Sweeney DA* *Superintendent Registrar.*

Deimhniú Breithe 🎵 Birth Certificate

Arna eisiúint de bhun an Achta um Chlárú Sibhialta 2004 — Issued in pursuance of the Civil Registration Act 2004

Éire   Ireland

	Cláraimhir Registration Number	10053682			Breith a Chláraíodh i gContae Birth Registered in the district of		Knocknalower
	i Imistár an Phriomh-Chláraitheora in the Superintendent Registrar's District of		Belmullet		i gContae in the County of		Co. Mayo

Uimh.	Dáta Breithe Date of Birth	Ainm	Gnéas	Ainm, Sloinne agus Ionad Chónaithe an Athar	Ainm agus Sloinne na Máthar agus a sloinne roimh phósadh di	Céim nó Gairm Bheatha an Athar	Siniú, Cáilíocht agus Ionad Chónaithe an Fhaisnéiseora	An Dáta a Chláraíodh	Siniú an Chláraitheora	Ainm E tugadh chld Breithe D
No.	Place of Birth	Name	Sex	Name and Surname and Dwelling-Place of Father	Name and Surname and Maiden name of Mother	Rank or Profession of Father	Signature, Qualification and Residence of Informant	When Registered	Signature of Registrar	Bap Name a Regist Birth
43	18 96 April Sixth Porturlin	Margaret	Female	Samuel McConnell Porturlin	Kate McConnell formerly Tighe	Farmer	Eliza Samuel & McConnell mark Father Porturlin	June Seventeenth 18 96	Henaghan Registrar	

Deimhnítear gur thiomnaíodh na sonraí seo ó chlárleabhar coinnithe faoi alt 13 den Acht um Chlárú Sibhialta 2004/Certified to be compiled from a register maintained under section 13 of the Civil Registration A
Eisithe ag / Issued by **Yvonne Hynes, Authorised Officer**   Dáta / Date Of Issue **11 May 2019**

Is cion tromchúiseach é an deimhniú seo a athrú nó é a úsáid agus é athraithe / To alter this certificate or to use it as altered is a serious offence

- 21 -

V S-60 (REV 1/78)

LOCAL REGISTRAR COPY

NEW YORK STATE
DEPARTMENT OF HEALTH
CERTIFICATE OF DEATH

RECORDED DISTRICT: 2901
REGISTER NUMBER: 207

NAME FIRST	MIDDLE	LAST	SEX	DATE OF DEATH
Margaret		MORAN	FEMALE	Apr 07 1987 5:27 P

AGE: 91 YEARS
DECEDENT BORN: MONTH 2 DAY 26 YEAR 96

COUNTY OF DEATH: Nassau
LOCALITY: VILLAGE OF Rockville Centre
HOSPITAL OR OTHER INSTITUTION: Mercy Hospital
ADMISSION DATE: Mar 26 87

STATE OF BIRTH: Ireland
CITIZEN OF WHAT COUNTRY: U.S.A.
MARITAL STATUS: WIDOWED

RACE: White
EDUCATION: indicate highest grade completed

USUAL OCCUPATION: Housewife
KIND OF BUSINESS OR INDUSTRY: Own Home

RESIDENCE:
STATE: New York
COUNTY: Nassau
VILLAGE OF: Malverne
STREET AND NUMBER OF RESIDENCE: 23 Carlisle Place 11565

NAME OF FATHER: James McDonnell
NAME OF MOTHER: Catherine Tighe

NAME OF INFORMANT: Mary Bennett
MAILING ADDRESS: 124 Cleavland Ave., Massapequa, N.Y. 11758

BURIAL, CREMATION, REMOVAL: Burial
PLACE OF BURIAL: 4 10 87; Holy Rood Cemetery
LOCATION: Westbury, New York

NAME AND ADDRESS OF FUNERAL HOME: Flinch & Bruns F.H. 34 Hempstead Ave. Lynbrook, N.Y. 11563

NAME OF FUNERAL DIRECTOR: Nicholas C. Fasano

TO BE COMPLETED BY CERTIFYING PHYSICIAN ONLY

—OR—

TO BE COMPLETED BY CORONER OR MEDICAL EXAMINER ONLY

FROM 3 26 87 to 4 7 87 4 7 87

NAME AND ADDRESS OF CERTIFIER: FLORENCIO A. GOMEZ MD 10 UNION AVE Lynbrook

DEATH WAS CAUSED BY
PART I. IMMEDIATE CAUSE
(A) CEREBROVASCULAR Thrombosis
DUE TO, OR AS A CONSEQUENCE OF:
(B) ATHeriosclerotic HEART DESEASE

INJURY AT WORK: NO
PLACE OF INJURY

NEIGHBOURS

Jackie O'Donnell
Porturlin

Father's name: John O'Donnell (Lacer)
Mother's name: Katie McDonnell (Jamesie)

They married and had 5 children in the family—3 boys and twin girls. John died at the very early age of 45.

My father, Tom and Eileen Flannery, neighbours to John and Katie, helped Katie out after the sudden death of her husband, John. Their son, Jackie, was like a son to my father, Tom Flannery (Sonny). Jackie went fishing at a very young age.

John and Katie, and Tom and Eileen's families, grew up together. They were like brothers and sisters to each other and good neighbours forever down through the years.

My father, Tom Flannery, would make poteen out in the mountains and Jackie would accompany him. After the brew was through, there was a party back at Jackie's house. Jackie's mother, Katie, was a good singer, and there would be a sing-song and some food, and the brew was sampled and everyone was happy.

Years later…

Years later, I accompanied Jackie in his car to a dance. He was picking up his first date with a lady by the name of Mary, who he later married, and they had their own family.

Jackie talked to me about his drinking, and he stopped drinking himself later.

Two years later, he was over in my house, and we were eating and talking, and he said to me, "I'm 2 years off the drink and, if I died in the morning, I die a happy man." His wishes to me was to build 2 rooms on to his house for his wife and kids.

Three days later, my mother called me. "Come down, there's something wrong with Jackie." And when I got there, they were taking him out of the house in a coffin. Jackie had passed away and I was very heart broken. I decided to take his kids back to my house to get them away from all the grief and sadness.

After his burial, I carried out his wishes. I raised 9,000 pounds and gave it to his wife. Jackie's wish was granted. The rooms were built. Thanks to everyone who donated and supported.

My grandmother was Catherine Tighe, and she married my grandfather, Tom Flannery.

My grandmother had a brother, Patrick (Patsy) Tighe, and sister Mary McDonnell was a sister to Catherine Tighe.

Patsy Tighe was related to McDonnell of Porturlin.

Mary Tighe married John O'Donnell, and she was a sister to Patsy Tighe and Catherine Flannery, Patrick's grandmother.

My grandfather was an animal person—loved his sheep and dogs, especially on the mountain. I think I followed on from him (Sonny) for his love of animals, something I inherited through my love of farming.

I had a dog for 20 years, called Enna. I got her for my daughter. but she remained with me. She would walk alongside me to the farm to tend the animals and wait for my return home.

If I was away, she would always have a welcome for me, meeting me at the door. Through the good and bad days, she was always there for me. When she died, it was so difficult. I felt I had no one to welcome me home anymore. I wrapped her up and buried her on the farm, marked by a grave and a cross reading, "My best friend for 20 years."

I met Dan O'Donnell in Belmullet. I told him of my loss of Enna. He seen the tears in my eyes and he said. "I see in you." He said that I was a lot like my grandfather, Sonny of Porturlin and his love of his beloved dogs.

Pat O'Donnell was from Porturlin. I called to ask for information on my grandmother and grandfather. The O'Donnells of Porturlin were second cousins.

Dan O'Donnell's mother was Baby O'Donnell, cousin to my father, Tom Flannery. We spoke about his mother—how kind she was to me as a child. I used to visit and work, boxing fish and looking after the sheep. She always rewarded me with 10 shillings. She would tell me not to say anything to anyone, so Tony (her son) would also pay me again (lol). She was also an amazing cook.

I told Dan I was treated so well when I was young. I always looked forward to meeting Dan and his wife for the craic. A lovely couple.

I received a phone call two weeks later that Dan had sadly passed away. I was very upset to learn of this, but memories of Dan and his family I will always treasure. Rest in peace Dan, and we will one day meet again and have the craic.

My grandfather, Tom Flannery, married Gannon of Killgalligan and they had seven children. His wife was expecting twins and giving birth. Both her and one of the children sadly died. The one son that survived was Anthony Flannery.

Years later, he met my grandmother, Catherine Tighe, and they had four children—Peter, Maggie, Pat, and my father Tom.

My father married my mother, Eileen Coyle from Geesala. They reared thirteen children. Tom Flannery, my grandfather was also known as Sonny. He had two brothers. His father was to divide the land in Porturlin between the brothers. The land was unfairly divided. He received the smallest parcel of land. He wanted his brother, Anthony, to receive the same amount of land, but he didn't receive anything.

Anthony later married a Tighe lady, and aunt of Sean Tighe, Carrowtighe. Both left home for Cork. I never figured out how long the journey took, but once in Cork, they got on a boat that took them on a three and a half month trip to New York, USA, and settled and started a life together. At that time, it wasn't easy. They had family there.

Anthony Flannery named his son after himself. His son met and married Winnie from Sligo. They were estate agents.

Anthony and Winnie had nine sons and one daughter (can see in pictures, USA). Anthony's family were in the US army and one of his sons, Brendan Flannery, was a pilot for the White House—an American government private jet.

Anthony traced his roots back to Porturlin. When I travelled to New York at 27 in 1984, I made contact with them when I worked there. I got on a train from New York to meet them and they met me at Old Saybrook. I was the first Flannery to meet them in the USA.

We embraced, hugged, and shed tears, and they took me to their home. On reaching their home, I was greeted by a big sign saying, "Flannery Row." Here they raised their family of ten children. Flannery Row consisted of just Flannery members, beautiful American-style houses. It had 150 acres of land—stunning.

I was so proud that my father's uncle, Anthony Flannery, who had left Porturlin all those decades ago had achieved so much and, to this day, that land in Porturlin with the family name through Tony Flannery. It gave me the courage to achieve things in my life.

It was true what a solicitor once said to me, *"If a Flannery fell from a ten story building, he would land on his feet."*

Flannery's Knitwear

It was in the nineties that I took to the road to promote and sell the knitwear on the road to knitwear shops. When I would be leaving Flannery's Village and I would fill up the boot of the car with sweaters and I would fill up the back and front seats of the car also with sweaters. It was all packed with sweaters. I'd hit the road and my first stop would be Newport. I was supplying two shops in Newport that I had got into. I would continue on then to Westport to supply another shop or two there and then I would continue on to Leenane, where I had another two shops to supply. I built up friends all over the place and then I'd go on to Cleggan for another shop, and on the way there was another shop between Clifton and Leenane. From there I went onto Miller's in Clifton. I used to be very nervous travelling to Miller's because when I used to try to get into the shops for them to buy my sweaters, they all opened their door for me, it took a lot of time and a lot to promote my knitwear - and to promote it as quality knitwear, that I was selling a good garment at a good wholesale price. It took a lot of time to convince them to do that and I didn't just run in and out, I built up time with these people. I remember that for three days before I would go travelling that I would be nervous as hell of Mrs. Miller because she was a very strict business woman. It was an honour to get into any shop but if you got into Miller's it was a big thing because most of the big companies were supplying Millers. So the first time that I went in there selling my quality Flannery knitwear, she said 'show me the quality that you are doing'. She was very exact but my stuff was quality and she bought it. She was very sharp, she wouldn't let anything go with me at all, if I was trying to explain to her about how good my knitwear was, she'd tell me that she knew knitwear, that she was in the business a long time "and you are only starting off." So she would always cut me off but as time went on, and even though I was nervous around her because of the way she used to be in the shop, I built up a good relationship with her too. She turned out to be a good lady and we used to talk. One day I was in the shop and when I was going around that time I always wore denim, denim jackets, shirts, I used to wear very eye catching shirts, I was more like an American - dressed with a lot of American clothes - and they were very eye catching.

One day I was in the shop and I was repeating orders with Mrs. Miller and the shop was packed out, and while she was doing business, you wouldn't go up to her and say "excuse me, can I talk to you, I have some nice samples to show you". It wouldn't be that, you'd have to make an appointment. I often waited two hours in the shop for her to see me. But I would wait, I had the patience. So one day I waited and she gave me the order for the sweaters, a big order and when I had finished, she was on about the shop and how the business was going. And she said "by the way, when you come into my shop again, you are no different than a tourist, the way you dress with your jeans and your bright eye catching shirts, and your denim jackets, when you come into my shop in future as a salesman, you dress up in a suit". So I said "yes, Mrs. Miller". And I left, when I went outside I said in my own mind "Fuck you". And I went off down the road to Roundstone. It was the late nineties when I got into the market in Roundstone and the first shop that I went into there was 'Kings'. When I went into the shop, of course I was dressed the same way with the denims and the eye catching bright shirt, and I did look like a tourist, so when I went into Kings there was a beautiful lady called Eileen in the shop. It was a very friendly shop, you could see that. I said "I'm from the tax office, I'm a tax inspector", just to break the talk and chat. The look that she gave me first and then she looked at my clothes and then she realised that I wasn't a tax inspector with the way that I was dressed! We got chatting and she ended up buying my knitwear, so I supplied knitwear - scarves, caps and socks - to the Kings family and we sat down and we had a cup of tea. Her mother came out and I got to meet all the family over time. That was the type of business that I was running. I built up a relationship with friendliness and I wasn't out to rip them off or they weren't out to rip me off either. We became good business friends and friends.

Then I would travel out to Joyce's in Recess - another family that had great time and respect for me. Then I would go on into Moycullen, into Tressa Garavan and they were the same way. We built up strong relationships as they were buying my knitwear. They would wait each year to give me orders and then I would go onto Tressa's sister in Galway city. And I would then travel all the way down through Tuam, all hours of the night travelling. But I realise today, in 2005, when I went back and visited all these shops and the people are still there, thanks be to God, and the shops are still open. But they never forgot the warmness, the minute that I walk into their shops, it's all 'Mr. Flannery, it's so good to see you'. The Kings in Roundstone had a great welcome for me, the big hug and the sit down and we had the tea and the brown bread and the chatting - we shared everything. They shared their lives with me. How their business was going, how their families were doing, if somebody was sick, that was shared and that's the type of relationship that I had with these people. I love Connemara, I loved everyone that I dealt with, between Galway, Connemara and the whole island, which I travelled selling and promoting Flannery Knitwear. Today, in 2005, they still want me back with the knitwear. I have been in the shop and they want me back early next year and they will give me orders again. And even though I don't supply them now, we still have the great relationships. The door is always open for me to go back into any of them shops, the respect they have and show for me and the respect that I show for them. They are able to tell me today too that Eileen in Kings in Roundstone is married and has three little kids now, showing me the pictures of them and the mother and the father were there. It's amazing, I'm so proud that I have done this with the knitwear, that I have travelled the whole country, meeting such lovely people like the Kings in Roundstone, like all the people that I dealt with. It's an education in life that will stick with me for the rest of my life - the warmness and the kindness - and yet we done business together.

I stayed in Roundstone last night, travelling around on a four-day tour. Most of the places that we are travelling to are shops and I'm looking up the shops that I used to supply.

When I started the knitwear first, I started out the knitwear in my garage onto my house, producing the knitwear, I had two knitting machines. When I was trying to get into the shops, they would ask me where my factory was. I would tell them that I had it in Pullathomas, but it was just a room onto my own house, a garage that I was working off. But at the time I couldn't go saying that I was working off a garage, it wouldn't look the part and I knew that I had to sell myself, to sell my products. You had to look the part. That's what I done and even one man said to me today "Jesus, all them years you had a Mercedes". I remember buying a Mercedes specially to sell the knitwear. It was a white Mercedes, the first one that I had back in the early nineties. They remember me coming up to their doors with the white Mercedes and it packed to the top with the sweaters. Them were great days that I remember. And the girls that I gave the work to at home, my ex-wife at the time, was working with the knitwear as well, pressing and labelling. It gave jobs to all them people. It was hard going through the travelling. I went into the shops and they might never have seen me before but within two hours I would have sold the knitwear.

I remember one time between Tuam and Galway there was a flower shop and I went in there talking and they were sorting the flowers out. It was just after starting up for a few years and within an hour and a half of talking to the lady there about how good she was doing, I started telling her that she would need something extra to boost her business and she asked me what. I told her that she would need something on the other side of her shelves to attract people in and when they come in to buy the something else, they will buy your flowers. In that time I had encouraged the woman to sell the Flannery Knitwear sweaters on those shelves. We turned out to be great friends after that and the knitwear and the flowers sold and she always told me that she couldn't believe that the sweaters and the flowers would sell together in the one shop because it was the last thing in her head. She was only into plants and flowers but that's the kind of educated business salesman that I became. I could sell anything! I loved people and I loved the road.

Then I was thinking about the machines going from half nine in the morning until one o clock at night in the garage down at home - it was booming. The pressing then was done in our own house and it was hard work but it was enjoyable - the workers enjoyed it.

Well we're still travelling, we stayed in Clifden last night and travelled around to all the people that I used to deal with throughout the years with the knitwear. We are still touring around now and we got the ferry to Kerry. We're going on to Tralee. We left home on Friday and we are gone into four counties already, just seeing the places that I used to travel with the knitwear. It's nice and the ferry coming across to Kerry is great, we saved two hours off the journey. So we will be travelling around for another few days. It's great to see all the houses going up everywhere in Kerry, the county that sees a lot of houses going up and the changes that's landed to Ireland in every county everywhere you go. It's the 26th August 2005 and it's great that we can do this - get away for a few days.

I built my factory in 1996 - the Knitwear factory - with the coffee shop and there used to be over one thousand in stock at all times there. And then after opening the factory I wasn't afraid to be telling the customers in the shops that I had a new factory for the sweaters. I invited them all down to visit us in the shop and pick out any design of a sweater that they wanted. That was a great achievement in itself, and then of course I built the holiday homes and then it all became Flannery's Village. When I travelled to America as well to sell the knitwear I invited the people that bought the knitwear to come and stay with me at the holiday homes for free. People were buying our stock from Chicago that time and it was the same way in Germany - I marketed the sweaters there as well and invited the people to stay again in the holiday homes. The people that came and stayed would order goods from me and we would send them on directly to them then.

I stayed in Tralee last night and enjoyed visiting the shops I used to supply. The highlight of the trip was this morning when I went to the Sinn Fein office in Tralee where I meet with my old comrade Martin Ferris, a person I know for a long time, a good Irish republican, and we sat down in the office and chatted about things and the way the government is handling things now. Up above the door of the office was *'Release the Rossport Five'*. We discussed their case and what would be the best way to get justice for them. He showed me some old pictures of troubled times and things that happened way back then. I am now moving on again with my tour, trying to cover as many counties in Ireland as I can. I have already been in four on this trip in August 2005. It's great to see the country booming, with building going on everywhere. There are beautiful towns in Ireland. We certainly have a country that we can be proud of and I'm listening to the radio this morning about Florida where they have a hurricane - hurricane Katrina they are calling it - where it's over two hundred miles per hour. How people are afraid for their lives there and here the sun is beating down on us today. That's the way the world is. We are lucky to be living in this country of Ireland and our climate is not bad when you hear about these hurricanes that other countries get.

I am now in Dingle, a beautiful town - a fishing town - in Kerry. I was off to see my Twinship - the trawler that I used to own - the Twinship. After leaving Dingle and going on Terbet Ferry, I will be heading back to Flannery's Village again, to my own base.

I also visited the McMullans in Sligo where they used to buy my knitwear as well. Annie Kate and her husband used to give me the first order around Easter time, and her order could be anything up to one thousand sweaters, it would take six weeks to get them ready and as soon as they were done, I would deliver them to her. She was a great customer and we turned out to be great friends as well. I still do business with them and we have the chat and the tea and the knitwear and she always says that I make quality sweaters - indeed I learned a lot from her and her designs too. Also Donegal town, I have friends there and in Killybegs and indeed all over Ireland and Northern Ireland that I used to supply with knitwear - I sold a lot of sweaters up there too and made good friends there. It is a part of Ireland that I liked visiting and still do today.

Patrick Flannerys Knitwear factory, 2001
Udaras Visit – Gus Ruddy, Paddy Cosgrove, Dr Kelly, Patrick Flannery, Udaras Na Gaeilg Galway Representative, Time Quinn, Mary from Connemara Udaras, Seamus O'Mhongain, Michael Healy.

Arriving in Knock

I'm landed in Knock and I have to get away to Charlestown because I left my car there on my way to Naas. I was looking around and I couldn't get a lift. I see these two fellas in a small van and I went over and asked them would they give me a lift. He said: 'Fucking walk it' and then he called me back and he said: 'You seem to be a character'. He was very drunk and he was very funny. I got in the back of the van and he asked me what my name was. I said: 'Patrick' and he said 'Mine is Padraig and who gives a fuck'. He saw the funny side of the story but the other fella was very weird. The fella that was drunk said to him: 'Come on, I have to get home to Achill' and he tried to start the van. But there were no keys in it, then he started looking for the keys and that was another half an hour of a delay. He said: 'I should have left the keys where I left them before, on the seat.' The other fellas were coming out with the funny stories about his drinking and he was after coming back from Germany. He told me that the other fella was very weird and he said: 'I think it's him that's drunk and not me'. So anyway we couldn't get the keys and the man didn't know what to do. The drunk fella said: 'I think I'll stretch my legs because it's pointless hiring a taxi like you' and he started laughing. He said: 'no fucking keys to drive it'. So he got out and looked in the driver's seat and he said: 'sure the keys are stuck in the ignition, what in the fuck is wrong with you'. They were there all the time and the other man couldn't see them. But anyway I got to Charlestown to pick up my car.

INTERVIEWS

Interview with Maria

I left Killala on the 25th April to go to Dublin with my friend Joey Greene and it was the fasted time ever that I was driven to Dublin. He's a car racer. It took us two hours to get to Naas. The reason for my visit to Naas is to see my daughter and she was entered into a beauty concert representing Naas at the Punchestown Festival. So we came to see Maria interviewed and the contest and she won it. I was so proud to be her father and to be there with her and my friend Joey Greene from Belfast. We had a good night. We stayed in the Naas Court.

I also visited the Wolfe Tone Grave on my travels.

I am just waiting for Maria to come down now to show me her prize. She's going to be taken around Naas and to the Racecourse for the whole week as the Queen of the Currach. So that was my journey to Dublin. Seeing Maria with the media around her, taking pictures of her, she will be on the papers. She is eighteen years old. A girl that knows what she wants from life. And she will achieve it. And my advice to her last night when I hugged her for winning was: '*Maria, you are going places and you will get places, but just keep your head cool'.* So it's a big celebration again today.

I'm just interviewing my daughter Maria about the night that she won the Ms. Punchestown Competition.

PF: Maria, how did you feel when you won?
MARIA: At the beginning of the night I felt nervous but I had my family and friends there to support me. So when I went up there on the stage I was good and I just acted naturally. And I think that's how I won.

PF: So what are you going to do now for the rest of the week? You are going to be involved with the festival for the whole week.

MARIA: I will, I will be in Naas to meet people and I will be introduced to Ms. Punchestown 2004.

PF: Ok and what was the pub you represented?

MARIA: Kavanagh's Pub, Naas.

PF: That's the pub that you work in part – time?

MARIA: Yes, it is.

PF: And can you tell me how you got the job in the Bank of Ireland?

MARIA: I met Kieran Redmond, the Manager of the bank through the pub and I asked him would he be able to help out in getting a job in the Bank of Ireland. So he told me to send in my CV and he would help me out and he did, I got the job that day.

PF: And how long were you waiting?

MARIA: Two hours.

PF: Are you happy working in the bank?

MARIA: I am delighted.

PF: So you have the old brains of your father.

MARIA: I don't know.

PF: So what are going doing today?

MARIA: Today I'm going over to the boss to see what I have to do for the week.

PF: So he'll give you the guidelines for the whole week and what you are doing.

END OF INTERVIEW

Interview with Michael Burke, Porturlin.

Well I am down here with Michael Burke from Porturlin, a second cousin of mine. We'll be doing a talk about the fishing and the way times were.

PF: Your father fished with my father, Tom Flannery?
MB: That's right.

PF: And were there boats that time?
MB: Ah there wasn't, that was the late fifties, in 1957, lobster fishing. Salmon fishing and lobster fishing.

PF: And was it currachs then ye used?
MB: Yes, twenty-two foot currachs for the salmon fishing, eighteen foot currachs for the lobster fishing.

PF: And it was hard work I believe at that time?
MB: It was, cruel.

PF: And would ye go far out fishing that time Michael?
MB: We would go out six to eight miles if it was calm. It would depend on the weather.

PF: And was the salmon plentiful that time?
MB: The salmon was plentiful that time but there wasn't much gear to catch them with. Five nets to each currach and five men in each and five oars.

PF: That would be like one hundred and fifty yards would it be?
MB: It would work out at about eight hundred yards, I think for the five nets and the way they had them mounted.

PF: Eight hundred yards. And how much would salmon be making that time in prices?
MB: Well I don't know…my father when was young was getting three to the pound.

PF: Three to the pound

MB: That would be the 1920's now, it's going back a long way.

PF: And what was Porturlin like as a village that time? Was it all fishermen?

MB: Yes, all fishermen.

PF: They wouldn't be but small farmers.

MB: A few acres each. There was only twenty-one houses in it.

PF: And what year did the first fishing boat come?

MB: In 1961, the first boat came to Porturlin and in 1962 then six more boats came and it went on then until all well I remember thirty-four being in it, fishing salmon in Porturlin.

PF: Ad was it twenty-six foot boats that came first?

MB: Yes.

PF: Would they have been grant aided then?

MB: They were grant aided by BIM.

PF: So did they catch more fish then?

MB: Of course they did indeed, twice more than they were getting in the currachs.

PF: And they brought in more money of course too.

MB: Yes but then again the market wasn't great either. They had to do with whatever they go, so far one and six pence a pound.

PF: Was it in the currachs that our fathers fished together?

MB: Yes it was of course. Well they didn't fish together but they fished in Porturlin, they used to fish lobster together alright.

PF: And what kind of pots did they use for the lobster that time?

MB: Pots made from heather off the mountains and the cliffs.

PF: They were handmade?

MB: They used to weave them like the way the baskets are made now, they were made in a different shape, round with a pipe in one end of them.

PF: And how many would they use in each currach then for fishing the lobster?
MB: They'd used twenty to thirty pots, some forty or fifty.

PF: And tell me Michael, Porturlin as a village, was it a poor village or was it because we were fishermen that we were better off than the villages that didn't fish?
MB: I don't know, you couldn't be that much better off because you only had the summer months. A few extra pounds for the year that you would do well on the fishing. But there was no big money so there wasn't.

PF: There was no big money made?
MB: Ah no, for a good few years after getting the boats, there still wasn't.

PF: But lads like ourselves that were brought up in Porturlin, we didn't have to go to England like other villages.
MB; Well we didn't have to go in the summer months, but maybe at back end some of them might for the winter.

PF: And they'd work the winter there.
MB: Yes, and come back again for the fishing.

PF: The fishing always brought them home. How old were you yourself when you started fishing?
MB: I was thirteen years old.

PF: And how old were you when you left school?
MB: I left the same year.

PF: So you left school at thirteen and went fishing at thirteen. And did you find it hard?
MB: No it wasn't, we were making money at a young age. The boats had engines so there was no rowing. And we didn't mind hauling in

the fishing gear by hand. Each man would give you a hand and we would take turns to make the work easier.

PG: But the hands would be sore for a while.
MB: Oh they would but you would get used to it, they would harder up and get stronger. When you'd weigh the fish in the morning you have a god glass of whiskey and two bottles of Guinness. You'd go home then and eat a good breakfast and sleep like a pig.

PF: And you would go back out fishing again?
MB: Back out again in the evening.

PF: And tell me about the drink Michael. Was it the men that were buying the fish at the time.
MB: They would buy the drink, but no one would go too far with the drink. Every man would have a drink in the morning.

PF: A couple of whiskeys?
MB: Each man would have a glass of whiskey in the morning and the two bottles of Guinness. They would be sober and they'd go home.

PF: So do you have good memories of Porturlin growing up Michael?
MB: Oh, I have.

PF: You were happy growing up in Porturlin?
MB: Oh I was, it was a great life with the fishing. There were summers here that there would be over one hundred men fishing there.

PF: That was amazing.
MB: And maybe up to one hundred and fifty some summers here.

PF: And people from out the village would come in and fish there?
MB: Yes, the outside villages, around locally.

PF: Michael what year was it the bigger boats again came?

MB: I would say 1970s, in the 1960s it was all the twenty-six footers, then in the seventies a few thirty footers came, and thirty-six foot and up to forty. Well it didn't make things any better then because the fish started getting scarce then. The salmon was getting scarce then. The bigger trawlers started fishing the salmon out in the deep so they weren't letting them in where the small boats used to fish them. The Donegal trawlers had it fenced off.

PF: So they didn't help the fishing around here?

MB: No, no they robbed it with all kinds of fish. It's like their own out there now there is nothing in it.

PF: The fish is gone out of it now.

MB; It is the fish is gone. Then the super trawlers took them as well. The coastline of Sligo, Mayo and Galway is finished.

PF: Its sad though because there was a lot of money to be made here.

MB: You would have to go one hundred miles now to get a fish. One hundred miles west, out in the deep.

PF: Tell me Michael when the boats got bigger, the fish were getting more scarce so I'm sure the crews started getting smaller.

MB: The did, they started out with four men, this was reduced to three men, some of them are fishing now with two. And even a few trying to fish with one person.

PF: They couldn't afford to pay a full crew.

MB: No, they couldn't afford it because if they are not getting any fish they are not making any money.

PF: So do you think Porturlin is worse off now than it was?

MB: It is for the fishing because the fish is so scarce. It's almost finished there now. There's only a few boats fishing crabs left now but they aren't making any money. There are more pots in it now than crabs.

PF: Its sad. Tell about the poteen. Do you remember it?
MB: On the poteen was good old crack. People used to make an odd drop for themselves.

PF: So they always had their own drink?
MB: Some would have. They didn't make poteen for sale or money, they would just make a drop for themselves.

PF: So it is a changed village now.
MB: It is, it's not as lively as it used to be when the fishing was good, it put great life in the place. Everyone had extra money to spend then sure.

PF: That's right. Do you remember the first car coming to Porturlin?
MB: I do.

PF: And what year was that Michael?
MB: Well I don't remember the first car because the first car was here before I was born. I think it was in the late 1960's that they started coming in.

PF: Then everyone had a car? And would that be because the fishing was good then?
MB: Oh it was, yes.

PF: And the road going into Porturlin, what year was it tarred first? I think I remember the tarring of that road. Would it have been in the sixties too?
MB: It would be in the late sixties, about 1967 or 1968. I worked on it.

PF: Did you work on the road too? In the winter time?
MB: Yes I did. It went on for two years I think.

PF: And who was buying salmon in them years?
MB: When I started Eamon Munnelly, Geesala, used to buy them and the O'Donnells would buy them too.

PF: And Brendan Doherty?
MB: Yes, and the Dohertys from Carrowgeige.

PF: They would be the three main buyers.
MB: They were. Sure they were paying as good as they could and as good as what was going at the time. Thinks were very cheap in the 1960s anyway. When you went into a shop, you would get an awful lot of stuff for five pounds or ten.

PF: So food was cheap. Do you think that when the fishing was good that there should have been fish factories put in and Porturlin to keep the fishermen there? Do you think that would have worked?
MB: I suppose it would have helped for a while surely. The way it would be that the factory would only last as long as the fish would last.

PF; But it would have been better do you think?
MB: It would have been better in them years for the village. They were the days that there was big money made in Killybegs, back in the sixties. There was a market for the herring and white fish. I remember when we were out fishing and you would look back at the water, you could see the herring under you. There were so plentiful. Schools of them, playing near the top of the water on a warm day.

PF: So you believe that the super trawlers did take the fish?
MB: I do, they cleaned it.

PF: Does it sadden you when you think of that too?
MB: It does of course. It was nice when you went fishing, for sure. And you were sure back then that you were going to get fish. But now you're not so sure. It's not worth going out and coming back in again empty, most of the time.

PF: But that fish was the main food that we ate, that there wasn't much meat.

MB: Not a lot of meat.

PF: And then in the winter you'd salt the fish like ourselves and you'd have a supply for the winter.

MB: We used to salt the mackerel. And a glass of poteen before the dinner and you'd eat a good dinner then. Salty mackerel and ten or twelve good potatoes and a raw onion. And you wouldn't want any more food for the day.

PF: Healthy food Michael?

MB: It was healthy and would sleep.

PF: Do you think people were stronger then than now and there wouldn't be too many with flues or sickness.

MB: The people were stronger and no sickness.

PF: Tell me how the people in the village got on, did they agrees with each other.?

MB: They did, agreed with each other very well.

PF: Was there jealousy amongst them.?

MB: Oh no jealousy or I never saw any trouble or any fight. They were great neighbours altogether, all running to help each other.

PF: Do you think that this generation has changed a bit?

MB: They haven't I don't think, they are alright yet, they are much the same way.

PF: But there are less younger people now.

MB: They are growing up, finishing school and going away to Galway and all the cities and those that don't, work around. There aren't as many going to England now as there used to be. When I was young people were going to England and America and all the girls went and never came back, only for holidays.

PF: Its different times now Michael. When you look back at them times and the fishing, were we better off then than we are now? Were we happier then than we are?

MB: I suppose we were younger then anyway and its alright all the same.

PF: There is no one starving here.

MB: Oh no, and if there is anyone, it's their own fault.

PF: The houses now have changed and everything. Bigger houses now.

MB: Visiting was a great crack in winter time – the rambling houses. And you had the card playing in the houses, twenty-five.

PF: Would that be five nights a week?

MB: It would be. Then Saturday night and Sunday night we would go to the pub and to the dances.

PF: How many dances would you go to?

MB: There used to dances on Saturday nights and Sunday nights one time when the Palm Court opened in the 1970s where the Web is now.

PF: So there were more things happening in Erris at that time?

MB: I don't know because there seems to be good crack all the time around Belmullet. Of course we are twenty-two miles out from Belmullet. And the drink driving is playing hell. The police have stopped the crack, everyone is afraid to have a drink.

PF: But do you remember PJ Garvins hall?

MB: I don indeed, it used to be good.

PF: Would there be one dance a week there?

MB: No there might be two dances a month. All the big nights then around Christmas time, St. Patricks Day and Easter and all them.

PF: And big crowds?

MB: Yes and big bands, good bands, good ceilí bands.

PF: Did he run pictures in it then as well?

MB: He did in the winter time and the priest used to have socials there as well.

PF: What do you remember about going to school Michael? Was it Porturlin school that you went to? Who was teaching at that time.?

MB: Yes, Porturlin School. When we went to school first I think it was Peggy Doherty, Carrowteige. And then a Mrs. McGuire from Crossmolina, Ms. Gardiner then from Ballycastle was there as well.

PF: And were they qualified teachers?

MB: They were. The education back then was just to read and write.

PF: But when you left school you were able to do that?

MB: Well, not great at it. The girls had a bit more heed on the education but the boys were fishing.

PF: So when you left school, was there any of your class mates that couldn't read or write?

MB: I suppose there would be a few.

PF: But they didn't mind because they were fishermen.

MB: But they taught themselves again after that. The papers, the newspapers, the Western People was a great paper for learning how to read. If you kept reading it every week you would be learning new things every week. It was slow but sure. You would get some help with it.

PF: But in them times there wouldn't be much worry on people as there is now though. There was less pressure then.

MB: Ah not as much worry and pressure.

PF: The schooling is a big thing now in Ireland.

MB: It is, education is the main thing. If you don't have your education now you have nothing. Worse than an ass.

PF: Remembering back to them days again, was there two shops in Porturlin?
MB: There was.

PF: So you could get everything that you wanted there?
MB: Oh yes, everything was in them.

PF: Do you remember dealing with the shop keeper at the start of the salmon season, and everything could be put in the book until the end of the season?
MB: If you didn't have the money, they would give you what you wanted until the fishing season was over.

PF: And everything cleared up again?
MB: Oh yes, the fishermen would clear the books then.

PF: It was a way of life then that way?
MB: It was, things were scarce in the sixties. An awful lot of places had to close up for the summer and go to England or Scotland picking potatoes to gather a few pounds for the winter.

PF: I'm sure you put in bad at nights at sea too?
MB: There was some bad nights alright. And bad days. Rough seas.

PF: Was there any time that you thought that you wouldn't make it back into shore?
MB: No there wasn't.

PF: You always kept the faith?
MB: I did and were used to it. You would know when it would be too rough and you would haul up the gear and go home. It was better.

PF: Do you think that Porturlin was lucky in the line of deaths at sea?
MB: It was thank God, there was no drowning. I suppose they used to look for it because they took chances when it wouldn't be fit.

PF: Would they a drop of whiskey with them in the boats?

MB: No, I never seen whiskey on the boats or anyone drunk going out either. They were careful like that now. And if they had a small drop in self they wouldn't abuse it.

PF: So any other memory of Porturlin Michael?

MB: No not really, just going to school and coming from school and that's all. Going to school with a sod of turf under your arm for the open fire at school, for the teachers. That small school down in Porturlin I remember eighty-two kids going to it, which was a lot for a small school and there were only two villages really, Porturlin and Ryanatogger??

PF: That was a lot of kids.

MB: It was.

PF: I remember walking in the feet in the summertime. Did you?

MB: We would be in the feet in the summertime. They'd be no shoes.

PF: But you would have the shoes if you wanted them?

MB: You would but once one person was in their feet, everyone went in their feet in the summertime.

PF: Then in the summer, when you would come home from school, there would be the saving of the turf.

MB: Yes, everyone went to the bog that time and saved the hay. Everyone had their own supply. Everyone had their own potatoes, their own vegetables, their own fish, their own cows and milk sure.

PF: Every house in Porturlin?

MB: Yes.

PF: Do you remember them killing the sheep?

MB: I do indeed.

PF: You wouldn't be buying from the butchers then?
MB: No.

PF: So with the fishing and the small bit of arming in Porturlin they would be able to survive.
MB: They were, yes. They survived winter times. And according to what we were told not one died the time of the famine in Porturlin with hunger. The cause of the hunger was that no potato grew during famine years and the same thing happened in Porturlin with the potatoes but the fishermen survived on fish.

PF: Amazing. Would you say that you had a happy childhood?
MB: It was. I would do it all over again.

PF: Do you mind me asking you how old are you now?
MB: I am fifty-five.

END OF INTERVIEW

Interview with Pat O'Donnell, who is from Graughill but left there many years ago and Anthony O'Donnell, his brother.
The interview is telling the story about what it was like to grow up in Graughill in them days.

PF: What was it like for you growing up in Graughill as a kid?
POD: Exciting in a primitive type of a way. We got together a lot.

PF: When you compare them times with today, do you think that they were hard times?
POD: They were hard times, a lot of hardship but we were never hungry. We always had a bit of fish, bread, potatoes and a pig for a bit of meat.

PF: So you had all your own food?
POD: We had all our own food, and it was all provided from a little piece of land.

PF: And what would you be talking about? About nine acres of land
POD: Yes, about eight or nine acres of land.

PF: How many kids were in your family?
POD: There were seven children in the family and everybody got on well together. We were all a very happy family and I have great memories of it. Christmas dinner was the big day, once a year. But my father used to go to England in them days for the summer and my mother did the work.

PF: And the women worked very hard in them days?
POD. Very hard. The cooked all the bread, made all the meals, spun all the wool and made sweaters and socks. Washed the clothes by hand, milked the cows, fed the cows, and fed the hens.

PF: They were marvelous people.
POD: Very hard, harsh work. Carried the potatoes from the field on their backs on a creel.

PF: Did everyone in the village do the same thing, as a family?
POD: Every family in the village practically lived in the same manner and did the same thing.

PF: And were ye all in the house? Do you remember your mother telling you?
POD: Three of the children were born at home here and there were four born in America.

PF: Your father went to America?
POD: My father and mother went to America on the 23rd November 1923.

PF: And what was America like then for the families that moved out there?
POD: It was harsh, very harsh.

PF: Was it a bit better than staying here?
POD: I don't think it was any better, in fact I think that it may have been harsher over there. For a few years things were very good but then they had the Wall Street Crash in America and the depression. It was very, very hard, especially for migrants.

PF: So things weren't great over there?
POD: Things were not great over there for migrants at that time. There was very little for them.

PF: Do you remember in Graughill the cargo ships coming in with food? I've been told about the currachs rowing out to get wine and drink and food off them?
POD: Oh sure I remember when the Spanish trawlers came in, we'd get a couple of hens or ducks then we'd go on and get some brandy or whiskey or whatever, we would trade them.

PF: And would they give ye fish at the time?
POD: Fish wasn't what the villagers wanted. They wanted a little bit of spirits.

PF: To do a bit of partying and drinking?
POD: A little bit of spirits for the party.

PF: And how did the neighbours in Graughill get on? Did they all agree with each other or were they jealous of each other at that time?
POD: My recollection of it was that there would be very little agreement amongst them. There was always animosity among the neighbours and feuding over petty stuff, unfortunately.

PF: Like over lands?
POD: Over a little bit of land or a little bit of bog, who had one cow more than the other one, and all that type of stuff. There was always that in the village. There was feuding over the cattle going into another person's land, or sheep or the dog chasing the wrong cow or whatever it may be. It was very petty type of stuff.

PF: Would the neighbours all fall out with you over that? Would they stop talking to each other over that?
POD: Well my recollection would be that some of the neighbours were not friendly to each other. But most of the children got on well together.

PF: The kids got on alright?
POD: Most of the time.

END OF INTERVIEW

INTERVIEW WITH ANTHONY O'DONNELL

PF: What was the experience like for you Anthony growing up in Graughill?
AOD: Well there not too much that I can add to what my brother Patrick already said, except about the women. They would also be down on the shores with the creels on their backs, bringing up the seaweed to put on the meadows.

PF: That was the manure that they used to put on the land. How old were you when you left Anthony?
AOD; I was sixteen when I left here.

PF: But you kept coming back every year?
AOD: For the first couple of years and then I got sort of lost in the wilderness.

PF: Made your own life over there?
AOD: Made my own life, yes.

PF: What was the fishing like? They used to fish with the currachs, I believe, at that time?
AOD: They used to fish with the currachs.

PF: So they kept themselves going on the fish as well there.
AOD: They were out in the currachs regularly. They used to catch the fish and put them in a wooden barrel and salt them and you always had a bit of fish.

PF: For the while year around?
AOD: For the while year round. The would also kill a cow or a pig and the same things, salt it and soak it.

PF: So the money was scarce but at least they had their own food.
AOD: They lived off the land; they lived off the chickens mostly. They'd sell the eggs and buy groceries with the money, they'd buy a ten stone bag of flour at the time.

PF: What year would that be now Anthony?

AOD: Well I left in 1947, so that would be in the 1930s and 1940s.

PF: So the women worked very hard? The mothers worked very hard?

AOD: The did. They were doing the house work and the field work and a combination of two.

PF: When ye were young what leisure activated had ye? Used ye be at dances or were the dances in the house?

AOD: There used to be dances at the houses, we used to have here in the house in Graughhill, one a year.

PF: Once a year?

AOD: Yes, once a year. It would be chock a block and the money made out of it would go a long way towards buying clothes and different things, shoes for the kids. When we wore them, we didn't wear shoes very often.

PF: Ye were in yer feet?

AOD: Yes, we were in our bare feet. You would bring a couple of sods of turf with you under your arm down to the school to keep the school fire burning.

PF: And the school dances, they were called?

AOD: The school dances, yes, they were traditional. The used to run for two weeks for two shillings. There would be a piece of bread and jam and a cup of tea thrown in for that as well.

PF: And did you walk?

AOD: Well you walked everywhere. There wasn't a bicycle about then.

PF: Do you remember ever walking to Belmullet from here?

AOD: Oh God, dozens and dozens of times.

PF: And that eight miles?

AOD: There used to be on man in the village, I forget who it was now, and he had a bicycle and they'd be five or six of us running behind the bike into Belmullet and you would do the same coming back at night, run back again behind the bike.

PF: So the cows, fish and chickens would be sold in Belmullet at the fairs?
AOD: The cows yes, they would always take in a cow or a young calf and sell them. It used to be the 15th, the 15th of August was the big fair...The labha.

PF: Your father too would have worked hard at the time?
AOD: Oh definitely, if you are bringing up seven children, you've got to work pretty hard.

PF: And there were always big families at the time?
AOD: Always big families, always six or seven children.

PF: And what about girlfriends in them days? Were they like now, the dances were all virgins then?
AOD: The girlfriend's side of things, we were probably too young to mess with girls at fifteen or sixteen.

PF: There were no such things as going out, girls going out.
AOD: The parents were very strict on them. They wouldn't come in late, if you were visiting they would shout 'Home and go to bed' and you didn't answer back.

PF: Your obeyed your parents?
AOD: Oh you did yeah.

PF: Do you remember if the girls got pregnant at the time?
AOD: I can't remember of any girl here in Graughill or around the area that I know of that got pregnant.

PF: What would your reflection of the Graughill people, as neighbours be? Were they friendly people or were some of them fallout out with each other?
AOD: They'd have little arguments and forget about it because

when you'd be reeking your hay, all the neighbours would come and help out and vice versa, when it was their turn. And cutting the turf was the same, most of the neighbours would go around and cut one man's turf one day and carry on to somebody else the next day.

PF: Do you remember your parents talking about the 'Battle of the Boithrín'? Where the people were killed, Mary Deane?
AOD: No, not really.

PF: That was kept kind of quiet, wasn't it?
AOD: Well yes, I never heard them going back into history much.

PF: Back to Pat O'Donnell again now. Do you remember any ladies getting pregnant here at the time?
POD: Not in my memory, but it was brought to my memory. I had an aunt that got pregnant and immigrated to America that had a baby in Graughill and she never did return probably because of that reason.

PF: It was a big shame?
POD: It was horrible. I don't know if that was the reason that she never returned but she never did come back. But I do know that she had a baby, it was a kind of a tragic thing when that happened in them days.

PF: Would you think people were odd that time? Why were the people ashamed of these things?
POD: They were ashamed about having a baby without being married because I think a lot of that had to do with religion or church or upbringing. They were odd that way. They were also very odd about having autistic children or children with special needs. They kept them in their homes and were never exposed to the public. That was very odd and strange. So yes they had primitive ways a lot of them.

PF: Would you think today looking back on these times, was it a lack of education? It you look at today we are not ashamed of these things today, it's a gift today from God.

POD: It was the lack of education and dictatorship from the church. I think the church dictated to the people how to live their lives in them days.

PF: Tell me what it was like going to school for you. Were the teachers hard?

POD: They could be quite pleasant at times but they could also be very harsh and abusive to children. I never experienced it much myself because I didn't have a problem with whatever learning I had but there are children out there who cannot learn very well so the teachers were abusive who cannot learn very well so the teachers were abusive to them.

PF: At the time when I was going to school, I left school at ten and a half and I could never read or write. There was a big dunce cap put on me and I'd be behind the blackboard. Was that the type of attitude in your time as well? That if you couldn't read you were considered thick?

POD: I don't have any recollection of it because as I said I could read and write. I have a recollection of children who were not able to read or write or learn very well, were not treated properly, they were treated harshly at times.

PF: I'll go back to Anthony again. So Graughill for you growing up was a hard time?

AOD: It was a hard but happy times. I couldn't really remember of anyone being unhappy. People worked to survive and they were very, very friendly, most people anyway. Of course you would get the odd one. The ignorant person putting a cow over the fence eating the neighbouring grass.

PF: Your brother, God rest him Johnny, how old was he when he came back from America to take over the farm?
AOD: I'd say it was 1931

PF: I remember Johnny, when I came here to Graughill, and that's twenty-eight years ago and himself and his wife Kathleen were very good neighbours to me. They were one of the families in Graughill that welcomed me to Graughill. I remember being in Graughill when I was nine years old too and the neighbours used to go down with the carts in the night bringing up seaweed. But even as a kid I remember some of them even if they filled more or they had a bigger cart they were kind of jealous of each other, I thought at the time. And some of them didn't speak to each other at the time?
AOD: Well they didn't, I guess they didn't like strangers coming into the village, I'll be honest with you and you had to through that I suppose.

PF: I did, I did.
AOD: It always has been like that in Graughill. They didn't like that and my father had big problems too because he was from Aughoose.

PF: And they didn't accept him?
AOD: No they didn't, not at first. But eventually they became friendly with him and at the end of the day they had to accept him.

PF: But they find it hard to accept any outsider at all and I think that that is still here today too. So we'll move on, did you fish Anthony?
AOD: Oh yes, I used to be out in the currachs fishing mackerel, then take them on the back of the donkey and sell them around the local villages from the back of the cart. It was another way of earning a little extra money. It was part of living in them days. We accepted things the way they were and got on with their lives.

PF: I'll go back to Pat again about you brother Johnny, how many kids did he have?
POD: Seven.

PF: Seven kids, God bless them. And your brother died when he was young?
POD: Fifty-one when he died.

PF: And his wife Kathleen died shortly after that?
POD: She died at forty-five.

PF: I'm sure that you remember all that sadness.
POD: Oh sure, I was in America at the time of course but I do remember it very well.

PF: The kids are all grown up now, thank God.
POD: The children are all doing fine, there are four of them in London area, one married in Brighton with three children, the oldest boy John is with the Irish army, and he's a sergeant in the Irish army for over twenty years. One of the girls has just come back from England and bought a home around Ballaghadereen. They are all grown up and doing very well.

PF: When Johnny died and Kathleen, I remember that they were a very close couple. They were the closes couple that I ever remember and even to this day because when I came to Graughill they were the ones that welcomed me and we had only one kid and they'd let us out on a Saturday night because we were young, twenty at that time and Saturday night was their night and they gave us milk at the time and stuff like that. But how many years were between Johnny and his wife dying because I remember that was very close. Was it six months or five months at the time, can you remember or was it a year?
POD: Three, four or five months.

PF: Yeah I remember that there wasn't much in it. And the kids how old were the youngest and the oldest?
POD: The youngest was three and the oldest was sixteen.

PF: She died of heart break really?
POD: Well she had a cancerous tumor in her head probably brought on by the loss and stress. Sometimes cancer is brought on that is there but may lay dormant for many years but stress brings it on and I think that the loss of her husband brought that cancer on.

PF: Your old house is still standing there, what it like when you go up to that house now and look at it does it bring back memories all the time to you?
POD: It brings back the good memories, I don't think of the sad memories, I think of the joyful memories. We had a lot of happy times there. I never look for the sadness. I look on the positive side of it and the happiness and the joys that we had in that old house and the surroundings.

PF: would you like to come here to live in Graughill?
POD: No I'm too long in America now. And my children are there so I wouldn't move back. I love Ireland but I don't think that I could come back to live in this area.

PF: Did we change any bit? Or did we get worse?
POD: Oh yes, the changes are great. Some people don't think that they are but I think that they are great.

PF: Do you remember the pub down the road, Joe McGrath?
POD: Oh yes I do.

PF: And what did you think of Joe as a character?
POD: Joe was quite a personality, he had none. And I don't think he had much character either. But he never did me any wrong.

PF: He was a tough business man, yeah? Would you think that he was a good business man?
POD: I would give him zero for a business man.

PF: But yet people went into him though?

POD: Because they had no other place to go.

PF: Tell me how long you are working in the pubs in New York; you must be a long time in the pubs?

POD: Forty-five years working in the pubs in New York.

PF: Doing bar work?

POD: Yes.

PF: And still today?

POD: And still today.

PF: So you don't mind me asking you Pat, how are you today?

POD: Seventy-two and I still work five days a week.

PF: Well you don't look it. And your kids are reared and they are nearby and all that.

POD: Well one is in Vegas but not too far away really.

PF: I'll turn back to Anthony now. Do you remember Joe McGraths, the publican down the road?

AOD: I remember him well.

PF: Do you remember the old pub? I was told about the old pub, I don't remember it though they were telling me about it.

AOD: Neither do I but I drunk there and he had to take me home in the car.

PF: Is that right?

AOD: Yes, that's true.

PF: And what the old pub like?

AOD: It was like the usual pubs in them times. Sometimes you could drink there all day and other times they would just throw you out and they'd let you back in again.

PF: Would they put you out if you got drunk?

AOD: Well they'd clear the place if there looked like there was going to be a bit of trouble. If the trouble makers weren't in you'd stay outside and you'd go back in there and you could stay there all night, it would depend on what mood they were in.

PF: When people got drunk would there be a lot of fighting?
AOD: Well if you didn't see a good fight ever y weekend, there would be something wrong.

PF: Is that right?
AOD: Yes, mostly between families about some sort of an argument that they would have had at home. They'd be a few scraps and they'd go in and shake hands and drink together again for the rest of the night.

PF: So they would forget about it the next day?
AOD: The would forget about it the same night.

PF: And they were good fighters? Were they able to fight? They wouldn't hurt each other too much?
AOD: Most of it was one bloke taking his jacket off and two blokes holding him and if they let him out he wouldn't fight at all, it was mostly to do with the action.

PF: What did you think of Joe McGrath as a character?
AOD: He used to serve me and once he brought me home, I didn't have a lot to do with him to be honest with you.

PF: The reason that I am asking about him a lot is because a lot of people mention his name. That he was fun to go to. I remember myself; to me he was a comedian with the things that he would come out with in the pub. He used to love see people arguing and he'd be telling them to shut up to frig and he'd throw them outside the door. He used to draw more arguments in the pub than stopping them.
AOD: Well yes, there was that about him.

POD: He was abusive.
AOD: I didn't get involved or encouraged him.

PF: But there were a lot of people around here that time. The villages had a lot more people than now.

AOD: There always seemed to be a lot of people in the pubs in them days anyways.

PF: We're in 2004 now and hasn't the population gone down an awful lot in Erris since?

AOD: Oh yes it has definitely. There is only four or five in each house now.

PF: You must find it a big change. Do you remember the first hall then, the first one in Erris?

AOD: Let me think, the first hall in Erris. The McAndrews had a dance hall there in Gortbrack, you also had a hall in Foxpoint. There was a dance hall there as well. A lot of them used to go to Aughleam, the other side of Belmullet to go dancing. And then of course you had Glenamoy.

PF: We're going back to Pat now. Pat I want to ask you about the women in them days. You said they worked very hard, which they did. I remember even in my time and I'm the next generation up to you, they weren't allowed into pubs? You would never see a woman in a pub.

POD: Well the women did not go to the pub. It wasn't that they weren't allowed, they just didn't go to the pub in them days.

PF: Was that the women's decision in them days?

POD: It was I would think. I wouldn't think that they weren't allowed, I would think that it was their own choice not to go to the pub.

PF: Going to mass in them days, tell me about the women. Could they not go into Mass without something over their head?

POD: Oh yeah, they had to wear a scarf or something over their head.

PF: Was that the church or was it their own choice?
POD: I think that was the church, it was the teaching of the church.

PF: And we'll say a woman in them days, would they wear a low neck dress? Or would they be allowed at the time? Would it be a long dress? Would they be allowed to wear a short dress?
POD: There wasn't that much low neck dresses at that time or short dresses.

PF: Your never seen any?
POD: No, not in the forties or fifties.

PF: There was a kind of restrictions on how to dress for the women?
POD: It was modest wearing clothes at that time.

PF: Because I remember when I went to school and that's a long time ago, thirty-eight years ago in the little school in Porturlin. I remember a girl coming in with jeans on her and it was the first time that I ever saw a girl in jeans at that time and the teachers put her out of the school because she wore them. I remember my mother coming up and gave out to the teacher over it. So there were restrictions on how you dressed at that time. It would kind of remind you now how things are in the Arab countries, how the women wear scarves around their face, would it remind you of something like that when you look back at it?
POD: It was a part of the old cultures of Ireland which were similar to some of the ancient cultures of the Arabs or the Indians in America.

PF: So our culture was a bit like that?
POD: Yes our culture at that time was a bit like that. Some of our old cultures, like the straw boys and the whaling at funerals and some of those things like some of the cultures that the Arabs and the Indians of America had and have.

PF: The funeral back them days, do you remember the, the funerals in the houses?
POD: Yes, very well.

PF: And did ye wait up until morning.
POD: Going to funerals as youngster s, especially if the person that died was old, a night of telling jokes and partying and wait up all night.

PF: Was there crying at this funeral?
POD: I never noticed anyone, we were having a ball.

PF: Ye enjoyed them?
POD: We were having a party. Free cigarettes, bread and jam, tea. It would be a couple of days of party nights out. I remember them well.

PF: Back to Anthony again. What did you think of the funerals at that time?
AOD: They used to have to keep the body in the house a couple of nights and it was called a 'wake'. We all used to go to the wake and we'd all sit around and Pat said have free cigarettes, free pipe tobacco, most of them then smoked pipes anyway. And then to the church, most of them wore shawls, black shawls. The men sat at one side of the church and the women sat at the other side. Men and women didn't mix in them days in the church.

POD & AOD: It was the same with the dance halls, especially the dances that the priest was at.
AOD: You'd have the men sitting one side of the hall and the women on the other side and you'd have to go over and ask them to dance with you.

PF: Did you think that religion was a bit too strong on the people? Or did it keep the families together? Was it a good thing when you look at today?
AOD: When I think back on it, it was probably a good thing. Maybe

it was a little bit too strict; they could have relaxed the rules a little bit.

PF: But did it keep families together?
AOD: I honestly think so.
PF: Marriages especially?
AOD: Yes, I think it did probably keep them together.

PF: Would you ever hear of a break up of a marriage in them days?
AOD: No, it wasn't talked about.

PF: When you got married, you married for life?
AOD: Indeed you did, whether it was good or bad you stuck with it. There were no second wives in them days.

PF: No

END OF INTERVIEW

Research on the family of:

Patrick McDonnell
of
Porturlin,
Kilcommon,
Co Mayo

January 2020

Introduction:

The Roman Catholic parish with which this research was concerned was Kilcommon Erris. Roman Catholic records for the parish of Kilcommon Erris commenced in 1860 for baptisms and for marriages. These records are available to the North Mayo Heritage Centre up to the year 1916 for baptisms and 1930 for marriages. The parish also maintains a death register, which commenced in 1922 and is available to the year 1932.

The civil registration of births, marriages and deaths for Roman Catholics in Ireland commenced in 1864. Records of births are extant to the year 1919, marriages to 1944, and deaths to 1969. The relevant civil registration district for this research was Knocknalower.

Personal and place names appearing in the research are spelled as they appear in a particular record. In all other cases, I have used the version of place names used by the Ordnance Survey of Ireland, and also the spelling McDonnell for the family name, which was occasionally recorded in local records as 'O'Donnell'.

Objective of the research:

The research sought to trace the whereabouts of the children born to your great grandparents, James McDonnell and Catherine Tighe. It also sought to identify the location of the family's landholding in the townland of Porturlin.

Research:

The earliest ancestor we can establish with certainty is **Patrick McDonnell**. He is your great great grandfather. Patrick was born c.1814.[1]

Patrick married Mary Fergus:[2]

---

[1] As per his age on his death record

[2] As per the pension application of Pat McDonnell (your great granduncle) dated the 01-Mar-1917

Patrick McDonnell married on the 09-Feb-1844 Mary Fergus, Kiltane. The witnesses to the marriage were Hugh Fergus and Bridgit Gallagher.[3]

After marriage, Patrick and Mary resided in Porturlin. Patrick was recorded as a tenant of William H. Carter[4] at the time of the publication of Griffith's Valuation of Tenements for the civil parish of Kilcommon Erris (1856).

This map, from osi.ie, illustrates the location of the townland of Porturlin in the context of north Co. Mayo.

---

[3] Kilcommon Erris R.C. Reg. Marrs., vol.1 p.32 417

[4] The Carter family of Castlemartin, County Kildare, inherited half the Shaen lands in the barony of Erris, County Mayo, through marriage with a Shaen heiress in 1750. In the mid-1820s they founded the town of Belmullet and developed it with the assistance of John Crampton, their agent, and the engineer, Patrick Knight. The Carters also owned the head rent of Corramore and Kilmore in the parish of Athleague, barony of Athlone, and an undivided moiety of Tarmonbarry in the barony of Ballintober, county Roscommon. These lands were offered for sale with other estates in counties Meath, Kildare and King's county (county Offaly) in May 1855. In 1876 the Carter family owned over 40,000 acres in county Mayo and had a residence in Oxfordshire, England. Lands, the property of Adelaide Shaen-Carter were sold in the Land Judges' Court in June 1885. The purchaser was John Conway. From landedestates.ie

Detail map of the townland of Porturlin. The location of the settlement during the 19th century is indicated in red.

This map, from askaboutireland.ie, illustrates the location (in yellow), of Patrick McDonnell's dwelling house in Porturlin in the decade after the publication of Griffith's Valuation of Tenements (1856).

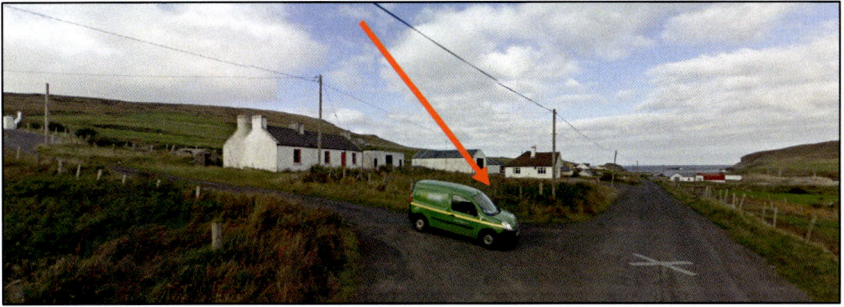

Modern street view of the plot leased by Patrick McDonnell during the 19th century. The red arrow indicates the approximate location of the old dwelling house. It can be reached via: 54.317116, -9.714151

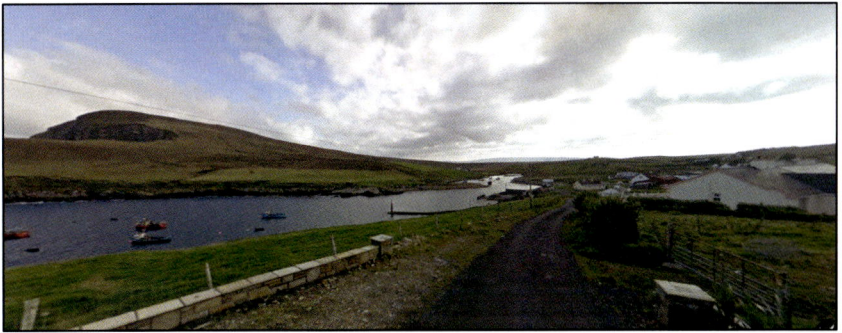

A view over Porturlin from the north. In the early 20th century fishing formed a large part of the local economy. The remote location of the village also made it convenient for the distillation of illicit spirits. There are many reports in local newspapers concerning cases brought against Porturlin natives for their involvement in this trade.

Patrick McDonnell died in 1894:

Pat McDonnell, Porturlin, a married farmer, died on the 01-Oct-1894 aged 80. The cause of death was probably old age, with no medical attendant. The informant to the registrar of his death was James McDonnell.[5]

Mary McDonnell, Porturlin, a farmer's widow, died on the 20-Jan-1897 aged 80. The cause of death was probably old age, with no medical attendant. The informant to the registrar of her death was Pat McAndrew.[6]

Patrick and Mary had the following known issue:

1. **Winifred McDonnell**, Porturlin, the child of Patrick McDonnell and Mary Fergus, was born c.1845.[7]

2. **Patrick McDonnell**, Porturlin, the child of Patrick McDonnell and Mary Fergus, was born c.1846.[8]

3. **James McDonnell**, Porturlin, the child of Patrick McDonnell and Mary Fergus, was born c.1849.[9]

4. **Anne McDonnell**, Porturlin, the child of Patrick McDonnell and Mary Fergus, was born c.1851.[10]

5. **Maggie McDonnell**, Porturlin, the child of Patrick McDonnell and Mary Fergus, was born c.1851.[11]

---

[5] Knocknalower District Reg. Deaths, vol.2 p.92 459

[6] Knocknalower District Reg. Deaths, vol.3 p.13 61

[7] As per the pension application of Pat McDonnell (your great granduncle) dated to the 01-Mar-1917

[8] As per the pension application of Pat McDonnell (your great granduncle) dated to the 01-Mar-1917.

[9] As per the pension application of Pat McDonnell (your great granduncle) dated to the 01-Mar-1917

[10] As per the pension application of Pat McDonnell (your great granduncle) dated to the 01-Mar-1917

[11] As per the pension application of Pat McDonnell (your great granduncle) dated to the 01-Mar-1917

We have no later records for Winifred Anne or Maggie. It is very likely that there were other children born to Patrick and Mary between 1851 and 1860, when the recording of baptism commenced in the parish of Kilcommon Erris. Further research can be commissioned from us to examine the life of your great granduncle, Patrick McDonnell.

Records concerning your great grandfather, James McDonnell (listed at no.3 on the previous page) are detailed here:

James McDonnell, Porturlin, a farmer and bachelor aged 30, the son of Patrick McDonnell, a farmer, married on the 16-Feb-1882 Catherine Tighe, Porturlin, a spinster aged 18, the daughter of Patrick Tighe, a farmer. The witnesses to the marriage were John McAndrew and Catherine Flannelly. The couple were married in Aughoose Church by John J. Melvin, P.P.[12]

After marriage, James and Catherine resided in Porturlin.

We do not have a record of the death of James McDonnell other than to state that he was deceased after 1927, when his daughter Maggie listed him on her emigration documents, and before 1941, when his wife was deceased:

Catherine McDonnell, Porturlin, a widow and old age pensioner, died on the 27-Oct-1941 aged 78. The cause of death was senile decay. The informant to the registrar of her death was Pat McDonnell, son of the deceased.[13]

---

[12] Knocknalower District Reg. Marrs., vol.1 p.714

[13] Knocknalower District Reg. Deaths, 1941, p.39 no.248

James and Catherine had the following known issue:

A. **Pat McDonnell**, Porturlin, the child of James MᴄDᴏɴɴᴇʟʟ and Catherine Tɪɢʜᴇ was born on the 20-Feb-1883 and baptised on the 23-Feb-1883. The sponsors were Pat Tighe and Mary Geraghty.[14]

   Patrick McDonnell, Porturlin, a farmer and bachelor, died on the 05-Dec-1954 aged 69. The cause of death was chronic bronchitis and asthma of several years' duration. The informant to the registrar of his death was Mary McDonnell, sister of the deceased.[15]

   Mary McDonnell was in fact Mary Flannery, but she registered her brother's death using her maiden name.

B. **Martin McDonnell**, Porturlin, the child of James MᴄDᴏɴɴᴇʟʟ and Catherine Tɪɢᴜᴇ was born on the 12-Nov-1884 and baptised on the 16-Nov-1884. The sponsors were Michael McDermott and Mary McDermott.[16]

   Martin was present in the family home in Porturlin in April of 1911. We have no later records for him.

C. **Winifred McDonnell**, Porturlin, the child of James MᴄDᴏɴɴᴇʟʟ and Catherine Tɪɢᴜᴇ was born c.1886.[17]

   Winney O'Donnell, Porturlin, a farmer's daughter, died on the 24-May-1888 aged 2. The cause of death was probably congenital debility, of 2 years' duration, with no medical attendant. The informant to the registrar of her death was James O'Donnell, father.[18]

---

[14] Kilcommon Erris R.C. Reg. Baptisms, vol.1 p.4

[15] Knocknalower District Reg. Deaths, 1954, p.39 no.242

[16] Kilcommon Erris R.C. Reg. Baptisms, vol.1 p.16

[17] As per her age on her death record

[18] Knocknalower District Reg. Deaths, vol.2 p.18 90

D. **<u>Anne McDonnell</u>**, Porturlin, the child of James MCDONNELL and Catherine TIGHE was born on the 02-Feb-1887.[19]

Anne McDonnell, Porturlin, a spinster, the daughter of James McDonnell, a farmer, married on the 07-Feb-1922 Patrick Tighe, Stonefield, a farmer and bachelor, the son of John Tighe, as farmer. The witnesses to the marriage were Michael Monaghan and Kate McDonnell. The couple were married in Cornboy by Patrick Durcan, C.C.[20]

After marriage, Patrick and Anne resided at Porturlin.

Patrick Tighe, Porturlin, a married old age pensioner, died on the 27-Mar-1966 aged 76. The cause of death was senile decay. The informant to the registrar of his death was Mary McAndrew, daughter of the deceased.[21]

We do not have a record of the death of Anne Tighe (*née* McDonnell). She lived for many years in Porturlin, with her brothers.

E. **<u>Neal O'Donnell</u>**, Porturlin, the child of Jas. O'DONNELL and Catherine TIGUE was baptised on the 28-Mar-1889. The sponsors were Thomas Tigue and Catherine Horkan.[22]

We have no later records of Neal. It is probable that he died in infancy.

---

[19] Knocknalower District Reg. Births, vol.3 p.35

[20] Knocknalower District Reg. Marrs, 1922, p.62 no.35

[21] Knocknalower District Reg. Deaths, 1966, p.43 no.149

[22] Kilcommon Erris R.C. Reg. Baptisms, vol.1 p.41

F. **Mary McDonnell**, Porturlin, the child of James MCDONNELL and Kate TIGHE was born on the 05-Apr-1889.[23]

Mary McDonnell, Porturlin, a spinster aged 25, the daughter of James McDonnell, a farmer, married on the 02-Mar-1917 John Flannery, Porturlin, a farmer and bachelor aged 28, the son of James Flannery, a farmer. The witnesses to the marriage were Michael Sheeran and Mary Murray. The couple were married in Kilcommon Erris Church by A. Timlin, P.P.[24]

| 581. | 2 roods and 31 perches of land in the townland of Porturlin and D.E.D. of Muingnabo. | Reps. John O'Donnell Reps. John Flannery Irish Land Commission | Nil | Reps. John O'Donnell Reps. John Flannery Irish Land Commission Kate O'Donnell |

The Connaught Telegraph, 05-Oct-1977 listing lands in Porturlin held by the family of the late John Flannery.

John and Mary had the following known issue:

i. **Thomas Flannery**, Porturlin, the child of John Flannery and Mary McDonnell, was born c.1917.[25]

Thomas Flannery married Ellen (Eileen) Coyle, a native of Geesala, Co. Mayo[26] in 1952.[27]

Thomas and Eileen resided in Porturlin after their marriage.
Thomas died on the 08-Jun-1987, and Eileen died on the 30-Jun-2003.
The couple are buried at Kilgalligan cemetery.

---

[23] Knocknalower District Reg. Births, vol.4 p.41

[24] Knocknalower District Reg. Marrs., vol.3 p.110 219

[25] As per the information on his headstone

[26] The Western People, the 22-Dec-1993

[27] Irish Index of Civil Marriage Registrations, Co. Mayo, Poor Law Union of Belmullet, 1952, vol.4 p.35

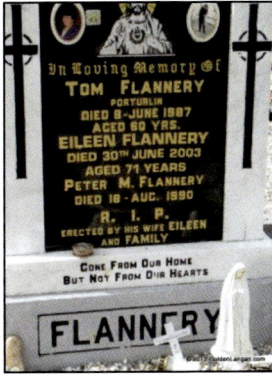

Image from goldenlangan.com

The Western People, 16-Jul-2003

Thomas and Eileen had the following children:

a. **Thomas John Flannery**, Porturlin, the child of Thomas Flannery and Eileen Coyle, was born in 1953.[28]

b. **Anne Rose Flannery**, Porturlin, the child of Thomas Flannery and Eileen Coyle.

Anne Rose married Plunkett McCann on the 14-Apr-1979:

The wedding took place on Saturday last at Cornboy Church of Mr Plunkett McCann, son of Mr and Mrs Robert McCann of Skreen and Miss Anne Rose Flannery, daughter of Mr Tom and Eileen Flannery of Porturlin. The Ceremony was performed by Fr. Noel Clarke C.C. Cornboy and the reception was held in the Kerryman's Inn Banagher.

The Western Journal, 20-Apr-1979

c. **Patrick Flannery**, Porturlin, the child of Thomas Flannery and Eileen Coyle.

d. **Andrew Flannery**, Porturlin, the child of Thomas Flannery and Eileen Coyle.

---

[28] Irish Index of Civil Birth Registrations, Co. Mayo, Poor Law Union of Belmullet, 1953, vol.4 p.53

Andrew married Kathleen Doherty in August of 1986:

WEDDING BELLS

A very pretty marriage took place recently at Carratigue Church between Mr. Andrew Flannery, son of Tom and Eileen Flannery, Porturlin, Carratigue, and Miss Kathleen Doherty, daughter of Mr. and Mrs. Doherty, Carratigue. The ceremony, with Nuptial Mass and Papal Blessing, was performed by Fr. Chris Ginnelly, C.C., Shanahee, and was assisted by Archdeacon Morrison, P.P., Aughleam.

Best man was Richard Flannery, and the groomsmen were Patrick and T. J. Flannery, brothers of the groom. Bridesmaids were Noreen, Geraldine, Josephine and Mrs. Martina Cafferkey, sisters of the bride. The flower girl was Cassie Cafferkey, niece of the bride, and the page boy was R. Wynne, nephew of the groom. Over 160 guests attended the reception in the Talk of the Town, Bangor Erris. The honeymoon was spent on a tour of the South of Ireland.

The Western People, 27-Aug-1986

ii. **Peter Flannery**, Porturlin, the child of John Flannery and Mary McDonnell.[29]

Peter died in Porturlin on the 18-Aug-1990. He is buried in Kilgalligan cemetery with his brother Tom and sister-in-law Eileen.

iii. **Pat Flannery**, Porturlin, the child of John Flannery and Mary McDonnell.[30]

Pat emigrated to England, and settled in the Lincoln area.

He died in Lincoln in February of 1984:

DIED IN ENGLAND

Sad news was learned in the Porturlin area last week on the death of Pat Flannery — a native of Porturlin. He died unexpectedly in Lincoln. He is survived by his wife and twelve of a family. He was brother of Peter Flannery, Porturlin, and sister of Mrs. Margaret Scanlon, Porturlin. The burial took place in Lincoln.

The Western People, 22-Feb-1984

---

[29] As per the information on his headstone

[30] As per the information on his headstone

iv. **Margaret Flannery**, Porturlin, the child of John Flannery and Mary McDonnell.

Margaret married (Unknown) Scanlon.
Margaret was resident in Porturlin in 1984.[31]

We have no later records of her.

G. **Thomas O'Donnell**, Porturlen, the child of James O'DONNELL and Kate TIGHE was born on the 14-Jul-1891.[32]

Thomas worked as a fisherman. The harbour of Porturlin opens into deep water which, while often dangerous, was historically abundant in fish.

Thomas McDonnell, Porturlin, a bachelor and fisherman, died on the 28-Dec-1950 aged 60. The cause of death was supposed influenza, of 10 days' duration. The informant to the registrar of his death was Pat McDonnell, brother of the deceased.[33]

H. **Pat O Donnell**, Porturlin, the child of James O Donnell and Kate Tighe was born on the 20-Jul-1892 and his birth was registered on the 08-Aug-1892. The informant to the registrar of his birth was James O'Donnell, father of the child.[34]

This child only lived for one month. He died on the 18-Aug-1892:

Pat O'Donnell, Porturlin, a farmer's son, died on the 18-Aug-1892 aged one month. The cause of death was probably a lump in the throat. The informant to the registrar of his death was James O' Donnell father of the deceased child.[35]

---

[31] The Western People, the 22-Feb-1984

[32] Knocknalower District Reg. Births, vol.5 p.2

[33] Knocknalower District Reg. Deaths, 1950, p.49 no.102

[34] Knocknalower District Reg. Births, vol.5 p.25

[35] Knocknalower District Reg. Deaths, vol.2, p.69 342

There is no clear reason, based upon the available records, why this child was named Pat when James and Kate already had a son of that name, who was born in 1883 and was living in the family home during the 1890s.

I. **James McDonnell**, Porturlin, the child of Jas. MCDONNELL and Catherine TIGUE was born on the 29-Dec-1893 and baptised on the 31-Dec-1893. The sponsors were Patrick Geraghty and Catherine Horkan.[36]

James was present in the family home in April of 1911. We have no later records for him.

J. **Margaret McDonnell**, Porturlin, the child of Jas. MCDONNELL and Catherine TIGHE was born on the 27-Feb-1896 and baptised on the 01-Mar-1896. The sponsors were John Geraghty and Mary Geraghty.[37]

Margaret emigrated to the United States in 1927. She departed Queenstown (Cobh, Co. Cork) on the 24-Jul-1927 on board the Adriatic, which arrived in New York on the 31-July-1927. She listed her closest living relative in Ireland as her father James of Porturlin, Ballina, Co. Mayo. She was travelling to her sister, Kate, who at that time resided on Long Island.

K. **Catherine McDonnell**, Porturlin, the child of Jas. MCDONNELL and Catherine TIGHE was born on the 22-Feb-1898 and baptised on the 27-Feb-1898. The sponsors were Pat Gannon and Mary Tighe.[38]

Catherine (Kate) emigrated to the United States. She was resident on Long Island, New York in July of 1927 when your grandmother, Maggie McDonnell arrived in New York.

---

[36] Kilcommon Erris R.C. Reg. Baptisms, vol.1 p.64

[37] Kilcommon Erris R.C. Reg. Baptisms, vol.1 p.71

[38] Kilcommon Erris R.C. Reg. Baptisms, vol.1 p.76

L. **Brigid McDonnell**, Porturlin, the child of Jas. MᶜDONNELL and Catherine TIGHE was born on the 21-Aug-1900 and baptised on the 26-Aug-1900. The sponsors were Anthy. McDonnell and Margaret Corcoran.[39]

Bridget was actually born in March of 1901. However a false date of birth may have been submitted to the registrar in order to avoid a fine for late registration, which was defined in law as 90 or more days after the event.

Bridget McDonnell, Porturlin, a farmer's daughter, died on the 22-Jan-1904 aged 3 and a half years. The cause of death was evidently croup. The informant to the registrar of her death was Patrick McDonnell of Porturlin, brother of the deceased child.[40]

M. **Unknown McDonnell**, the child of James McDonnell and Catherine Tighe, was born on the 06-Feb-1903.[41]

Infant O'Donnell, Porturlin, a farmer's son, died on the 06-Feb-1903. He only lived two minutes. The cause of death was probably convulsions, with no medical attendant. The informant to the registrar of his death was James McDonnell, father of the deceased.[42]

N. **Unknown McDonnell**, the child of James McDonnell and Catherine Tighe, was born on the 06-Feb-1903.[43]

Infant O'Donnell, Porturlin, a farmer's daughter, died on the 06-Feb-1903. She had only lived for five minutes. The cause of death was probably convulsions, with no medical attendant.

---

[39] Kilcommon Erris R.C. Reg. Baptisms, vol.1 p.83

[40] Knocknalower District Reg. Deaths, 1904, p.45 no.39

[41] Knocknalower District Reg. Deaths, vol.3, p.97 482

[42] Knocknalower District Reg. Deaths, vol.3, p.97 482

[43] Knocknalower District Reg. Deaths, vol.3, p.97 482

The informant to the registrar of her death was James Mc Donnell, father of the deceased.[44]

O. **John McDonnell**, Porturlin, the child of Jas. MCDONNELL and Catherine TIGHE was born on the 02-Apr-1904 and baptised on the 06-Apr-1904. The sponsors were Pat Tighe and Margaret Bourke.[45]

John was present in the family home in Porturlin in April of 1911. We have no later records of him.

---

[44] Knocknalower District Reg. Deaths, vol.3, p.97 483

[45] Kilcommon Erris R.C. Reg. Baptisms, vol.1 p.91

Appendix No.1: The Family of Patrick Tighe and Rose Deane:

Patrick Tighe married Rose Deane in 1928.[46]

The couple had one surviving child, Mary:

1. **Mary Tighe,** the child of Patrick Tighe and Rose Deane was born in 1928.[47]

   ### Mary Tighe married Martin McAndrew in 1952.[48]

   After marriage, the couple resided in Porturlin.

   Martin McAndrew died on the 26-Mar-1992, aged 70.

THE LATE MARTIN McANDREW

It was with deep regret we hard of the death of Martin McAndrew (70), Porturlan, which took place recently in Castlebar General Hospital following a brief illness. Martin's quiet unassuming and sympathetic nature was the hallmark of his character, he was a first-class farmer and genteel gentleman. He was regarded as a sincere person and a good friend. He was a manof high intellectual ability and one of the great loves of his life was the daily crossword.

He had a great love for children. Deepest sympathy is tendered to his wife, Mary, formerly mary Tighe,sous, Patrick, Brendan, Martin Joe and Vincent (Porturlin), Michael (Glenamoy), Philip (New York), Tony (London); daughters, Maureen (Galway), Rosanne (London), Margo (London), Pauline (London), sister, Mrs. Mary Davitt (York), sons-in-law,daughters-in-law, grandchildren, nieces and nephews. The

attendance at the removal of his remains and funeral on both occasions was very large and representative, and many people travelled very long distances, including London for the sad occasion, this was evidence of the esteem in which he was held. His remains were removed to the Star of the Sea Church, Cornboy, whre his remains were received by Fr. McHugh and Fr. McDonnell. Interment took place to Kilgallion cemetery, following Solemn Requiem Mass.

The Western People, 15-Apr-1992.

Mary Margaret McAndrew died on the 12-Jun-2007 aged 79. The couple are buried in Kilgalligan cemetery.[49]

Image from goldenlangan.com

---

[46] Information supplied by the client

[47] As per her headstone

[48] Irish Index of Civil Birth Registrations, Co. Mayo, Poor Law Union of Belmullet, 1952, vol.4 p.39

[49] Information from goldenlangan.com

Martin and Mary had the following children:

A. **Patrick McAndrew**, Porturlin, the child of Martin McAndrew and Mary Tighe.[50]

Patrick married Helen Naughton on the 28-Aug-1975.[51]

CORNBOY WEDDING

Cornboy R/C was the scene of a very pretty wedding on Tuesday, August 26th, between Mr. Patrick McAndrew, son of Mr. and Mrs. Martin McAndrew, Porturlin, and Miss Helen Naughton, daughter of Mr. and Mrs. Frank Naughton, Borhauve, Rossport. The ceremony, with Nuptial Mass, was performed by Rev. Fr. Brian Conlon, C.C., Cornboy. Best man was Mr. Michael McAndrew, brother of the groom. Groomsmen were Mr. M. J. McAndrew, brother of the groom; Michael and John Naughton, brothers of the bride. Bridesmaids were Misses Mary Doherty, cousin of the bride; Maureen McAndrew, Rose Anne McAndrew and Breege Naughton. Page boys, Vincent McAndrew, brother of the groom, and P. J. and Frank Naughton, brothers of the bride. Flower girls, Margo McAndrew and Pauleen McAndrew, sisters of the groom, and Geraldine Naughton, sister of the bride. The bride, who was given away by her father, wore a full length gown of white satin with full length veil held in place by a tiara of roses and she carried a bouquet of carnations. The bridesmaids wore full length dresses of pink with shoulder veils and matching hat. Over 150 guests attended the reception in the Central Hotel, Ballina, and afterwards the happy couple left to spend their honeymoon on a tour of Scotland.

The Western People, 27-Sep-1975.

B. **Martin Joe McAndrew**, Porturlin, the child of Martin McAndrew and Mary Tighe.[52]

Martin emigrated to London in 1979, he returned home in 1983.[53]

C. **Brendan McAndrew**, Porturlin, the child of Martin McAndrew and Mary Tighe.[54]

Brendan was resident in Porturlin at the time of his father's death in 1992.[55]

---

[50] The Western People, the 27-Sep-1975

[51] The Western People, the 27-Sep-1975

[52] The Western People, the 15-Apr-1992

[53] Information supplied by the client

[54] The Western People, the 15-Apr-1992

[55] The Western People, the 15-Apr-1992

D. **Vincent McAndrew**, Porturlin, the child of Martin McAndrew and Mary Tighe.[56]

Vincent was resident in Porturlin at the time of his father's death in 1992.[57]

E. **Michael McAndrew**, Porturlin, the child of Martin McAndrew and Mary Tighe.[58]

Michael was resident in Glenamoy, Co. Mayo at the time of his father's death in 1992.[59]

F. **Philip McAndrew**, Porturlin, the child of Martin McAndrew and Mary Tighe.[60]

Philip was resident in New York at the time of his father's death in 1992.[61]

G. **Tony McAndrew**, Porturlin, the child of Martin McAndrew and Mary Tighe.[62]

Tony was resident in London at the time of his father's death in 1992.[63]

H. **Maureen McAndrew**, Porturlin, the child of Martin McAndrew and Mary Tighe.[64]

Maureen was resident in Galway at the time of her father's death in 1992.[65]

---

[56] The Western People, the 15-Apr-1992

[57] The Western People, the 15-Apr-1992

[58] The Western People, the 15-Apr-1992

[59] The Western People, the 15-Apr-1992

[60] The Western People, the 15-Apr-1992

[61] The Western People, the 15-Apr-1992

[62] The Western People, the 15-Apr-1992

[63] The Western People, the 15-Apr-1992

[64] The Western People, the 15-Apr-1992

[65] The Western People, the 15-Apr-1992

I.   **Roseanne McAndrew**, Porturlin, the child of Martin McAndrew and Mary Tighe.[66]

Roseanne was resident in London at the time of her father's death in 1992.[67]

J.   **Margo McAndrew**, Porturlin, the child of Martin McAndrew and Mary Tighe.[68]

Margo was resident in London at the time of her father's death in 1992.[69]

K.   **Pauline McAndrew**, Porturlin, the child of Martin McAndrew and Mary Tighe.[70]

Pauline was resident in London at the time of her father's death in 1992.[71]

---

[66] The Western People, the 15-Apr-1992

[67] The Western People, the 15-Apr-1992

[68] The Western People, the 15-Apr-1992

[69] The Western People, the 15-Apr-1992

[70] The Western People, the 15-Apr-1992

[71] The Western People, the 15-Apr-1992

PORTURLIN - Port of the Foreshore

Area - 2,120 acres

Population   1841 -   110
                  1851 -   108
                  1911 -   139

1855 - Landlord: William Carter

Twenty dwelling houses.

This townland is situated three miles north east of Cornboy church.

On February 9th 1748, John Bingham of Newbrook, Co. Mayo, leased Porturlin and Shrataggle to Charles O'Donel of Newcastle, Co. Mayo, for thirty one years at a yearly rent of £28.5.0. They had formerly been held by Samuel Kirkwood. (225)

Within ten years of the surprise landing of the French at Killala in 1798 the English began building watch towers along the coast. A watch house, signal post, station house and coastguard station were built here at the beginning of the 19th century. They are clearly marked on the 1838 Ordnance Survey Map.

The finest fishing ground in Mayo is off Porturlin, wrote Richard Webb, who was here during the famine years to investigate the condition of the distressed for the Society of Friends. He wrote of this townland, "the only access by land is over a high and boggy mountain so wet and swampy that it is difficult to reach it even in Summer. There is probably not in Ireland a cluster of human habitations so completely secluded from easy access...... During my stay fishing was impracticable, owing to the severity and uncertainty of the weather. The mornings are frequently fine, and such as an experienced person would suppose suitable for the purposes of the fishermen, but towards noon the weather changes, the sky becomes overclouded and the winds blow with violence, and certain danger would await the frail currachs, or small boats that are employed in this coast, which is lined with cliffs ranging from fifty feet to five hundred feet in height. For about ten miles the only ports are the coves of Portacloy and Porturlin, and even these are not easily gained when a heavy swell sets in". (226)

Such were the problems of fishing for many years. Finally on March 25th 1886, Father Thomas Dolphin, Parish Priest, and Father John Colleran, Curate, sent a memorial to the Lord Lieutenant and Govenor General of Ireland with signatures of twenty two Porturlin people requesting a landing slip for the fishermen. (227) The landing slip, 210 feet long, was built within six months by the Roads and Harbour

Commissioners, costing £204. Sir Thomas Brady was in charge of the Roads and Harbour Commissioners at the time. (He was the husband of Annie Brady who contributed to the building of the old Muingnabo Bridge).

Further marine works were carried out at this port in 1909, when £71 was spent on repairing the pier and £3 removing rocks. At the time, £141 was spent on an approach road.

By May 1952, the old pier had fallen assunder, so it was replaced by a narrow concrete barge about two feet wide extending fifteen yards out into the sea.

Finally, in October 1965, Mayo County Council began work on a new pier a few yards away from the old one. It is about twelve feet wide, affording ample landing space for fishing nets, and accommodation for several boats.

A curing station for herring and mackeral was established here in 1894 by the Congested Districts Board. (228) Suitable vessels, fishing gear and a secure harbour are a necessity for fishermen. Unfortunately these facilities have not always been available. As early as 1835, William Bald, who surveyed this coastline, recommended the building of small harbours at Porturlin and Portacloy. He claimed that the fishermen had not the boats, fishing tackle, nor the skill for deep sea fishing. (229)

It was over fifty years before a landing slip was erected. And for a much longer period fishermen ventured out at night into the deep sea waters in currachs where they stayed for seven hours fishing, with little protection against the cold sea winds. Then, in the early hours of the morning they rowed homewards from as far away as Belderrig or Ceide. Their conditions were greatly improved by Bord Iascaigh Mhara when, in May 1962, twenty six feet long diesel engine boats with shelter cabins were delivered in the district. (230)

One can never under estimate the power of the sea and its dangers. It has taken many a life along Erris's rugged coast. William Bournes, Portacloy, wrote a song about five men who were drowned in Porturlin Bay. It goes as follows:

"It was on the 4th of April in the year of '78
A sad and sorrowful occurrence in Porturlin did take place
A crew of five in number went out at the dawn of day
But sadly they were drowned at last all in Porturlin Bay.

Those drowned on that sad day were Pat Cox, his three sons, and Thomas Tigue. They had gone out in the early morning to salvage timber, which they had seen floating in the bay. It seems that their currach capsized. (231)

Another drowning in this bay occurred about 1892, when two McAndrew brothers and a Tigue man were lost while lobster fishing. A vessel called the "Maid of the Moy" was wrecked here. The Erris Deep Sea Angling Club fish in this bay annually. During a fishing competition in 1972, Frank Brogan, Bangor, Erris, caught a halibut weighing 156 lbs, with a rod and line.

There was a pound in Porturlin. On February 9th 1836, a large party of men got together, broke down its walls and released twenty two head of cattle impounded for rent due to William Carter. All members of the party were known to the pound keeper. They were summoned to appear in court for the offence. The file on this case at Dublin Castle gives no information as to what the outcome was. (232)

The introduction of a road to this remote and secluded area in the 1840s was truly a blessing. In April of 1846, there was great distress all over Erris, and a great number were hurriedly disposing of their possessions and emigrating to America. The Justices of the Peace and other prominent men of the barony convened a special meeting in the Courthouse at Belmullet on April 20th and sent a letter to the Lord Lieutenant "for the construction of useful public works". (233)

A short time later, road making began under the Public Works Scheme. On September the 20th 1846, many works were sanctioned and approved. Among them was the making of a new road from Granny to Porturlin for which £200 was granted as a first instalment. On December the 7th of that year, £300 was granted to complete the road to Porturlin. At the same time, a grant of £175 was sanctioned to make a road from Geeverene to Porturlin. (234)

During the distress of 1895, Relief Works were again carried out in this townland, such as the repairing and making of roads and marine works. Men and women, boys and girls over fourteen were engaged in quarrying gravel and stones, and carrying the material on hand barrows, and breaking stones and building sod fences along the road. Work of this nature was done in several townlands throughout Erris. Men were paid seven shillings and sixpence per week, women six shillings and sixpence, and boys and girls six shillings. All those who lived over three miles from the works got threepence extra per week. Constable Jeremy Hegarty of Rossport was the ganger in Porturlin.

Maud Gonne, (Mother of Sean McBride, the Nobel Peace Prize Winner, who died in 1988) called to Porturlin in the course of her tour of the distressed. In a Press release later, she was strong in her condemnation of the Government for the way they were treating the poorer classes of society. She referred to Mary Naughton, a fourteen year old girl, who was working at the time on the roads of this townland.

There was a school house here in 1849. It is referred to in an application to the Board of Education from Glenamoy when the correspondent sought recognition of a school, salary for a teacher, and a grant for books. (235) This Porturlin school was never recognised or aided by the Board of Education.

A National School house (Roll No. 14843) was built for the people of this townland in 1896. The parish Inventory Book (1910) notes that the Porturlin National school "stands on a plot of one hundred square feet in the townland of Shrataggle and is enclosed by a wall. It is a rough-cast, slated building, with entrance hall and school room". (236)

In 1900, there were eighty pupils on the roll. Two Hegarty sisters, Maria and Katie, nieces of Father John Hegarty, taught here from 1901 to 1905. Later they taught in the Rossport National school. In 1902 their salaries were £52.5.0 when there were 94 children on the Roll. Evening classes began that year for persons over eighteen years. There were 38 men and women attending. Books were provided and the teacher received a slary of £28.10.0. At least two subjects had to be taught.

The Porturlin school closed on June 30th 1970. Since then the children have been transported to the National School at Rossport.

Father John Hegarty was instrumental in persuading the Congested Districts Board to establish a lace school here. He had a building erected. It was a corrugated iron-roofed house, built on commonage with the consent of the tenants. Here, lace and crochet classes were held in November 1909. Nora Mills of Gortmellia, an aunt of Michael Mills, the Ombudsman, was the lace teacher. She later married Anthony O'Donnell and settled here. After the lace school closed, the building became a residence for national school teachers. It was parish property at the time. Miss Cavanagh, a school teacher stayed here. It is now owned by Paddy O'Donnell.

The old age pension was first introduced in 1909. At the time there was nowhere nearer than Pollathomas where pensioners could cash their pension. It was with some delight, then, that they received news on October 1911 that two sub-post offices were to be established in the district, one at Porturlin and the other at Carratigue. In December 1911, John McAndrew of Porturlin was appointed sub-post master of the new post office. (237)

During the "Free Emigration" of 1883 the families of John Flannery and Peter McAndrew of Porturlin left Blacksod Bay on an Allen Liner for North America. (238)

Porturlin's beauty and grandeur are described by a writer to the Western People of June 29, 1895. He says "Let the tourist who may visit Erris leave himself a fine day for Porturlin. It will repay him a hundred fold". He talks of the beauty of a boat trip to Diamond Cave which he calls "Crystal Palace". Sea birds of every kind are found here. Excellent pictures were taken by English visitors of this townland and surroundings in 1894, copies of which were exhibited in the Royal Hotel, Belmullet, in June of 1895.

At the turn of the century Thomas Moran and his son, Michael, were weavers; Paddy Tigue was a boat and currach builder, and Patsy Walsh was an accordion player.

Appendix No.3: The Pension Application of Pat McDonnell (1917):

Con/S/2/, 1552

Application No. 2/17 1957.

Date of Receipt, 1. 9. 1917 Disposed of. ✓

EXTRACT FROM CENSUS RETURN OF 18

Full Name of Applicant, *Pat McDonnell.*

Address, *W. Pat McDonnell, Porturlin, Rossport Ballina Co. Mayo*

Full Names of Father and Mother of Applicant, *Pat + May McDonnell (Fargus)*

Name of Head of Family (if other than Father) with which Applicant resided in 18

Relationship and Occupation,

Residence in 1851 :

Winifred 6
Pat 5
James 2
Anne
Maggie

County, *Mayo*

Barony, *Erris*

Parish, *Kilcommon*

Townland, *Porturlin*

Street (if in a town),

Reside in 1851
Parent names
Head of
FW
5. 9. 17

£27-38

Place in Record Treasury,

Return searched by *JW 13/3/17 sheet 4*

Extract made by *WM 13/3/17*

Certified by *Jane 14.3.17*

Form replaced by *J.T. 14·3·17*

Copy despatched to Applicant's Address

15/3/17

(3693). Wt. 6003—16,10,000. 1/17 A.T.&Co. Ltd H.A.°

Family Photographs

*Patrick with his son Patrick
and granddaughter Nicole*

Patrick with his son Patrick

Celebrating a Flannery family wedding in Enniscrone Hotel

All dressed up with nowhere to go!

Kathleen with son Patrick

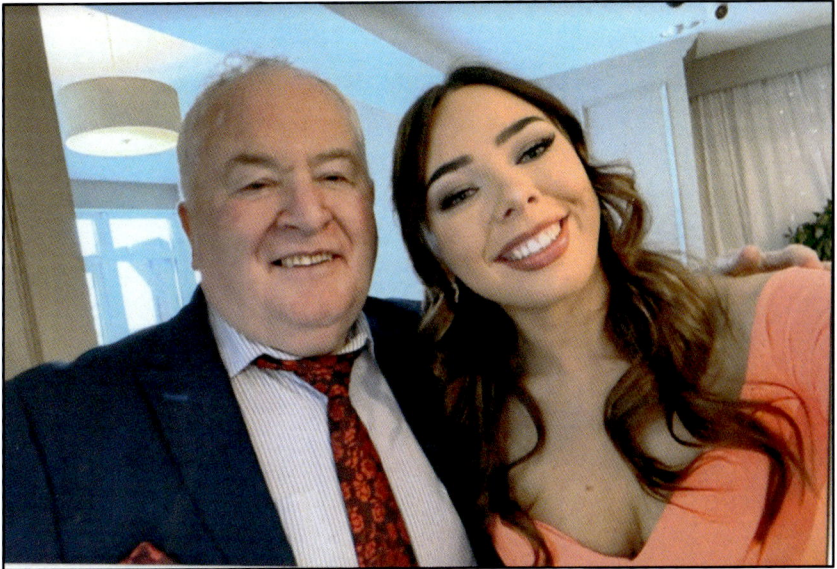

Patrick with his granddaughter Nicole

Jason Flannery & his wife on their wedding day
with Patrick & Kathleen

Patrick Flannery Junior with his Aunty Kathleen Flannery Barren. The aunty with a Big Heart.

Three generations;
Patrick Flannery Senior,
Patrick Flannery Junior,
Mark Flannery, grandson.

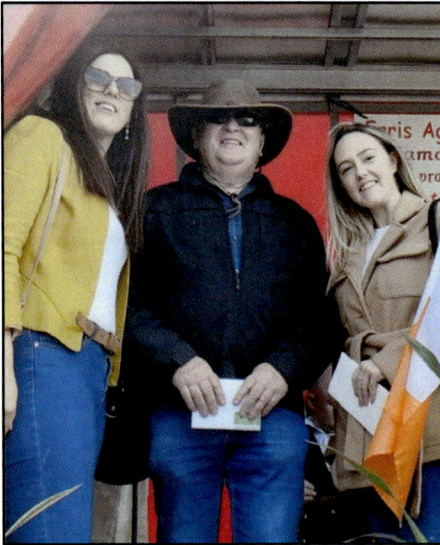

Patrick Flannery winning 1ˢᵗ prize at the Erris Agriculture Show

Patrick Flannery winning 2ⁿᵈ prize for his pen

My sister Martina's 60th birthday celebrations

Celebrating grandchildren's communion

Patrick Flannery with his children & grandkids celebrating Christmas.

Patrick with his grandkids Harry, Ben & Ruby on Flannery's farm.

Harry on his First Holy Communion Day at his home.

Grandson Shane and his friend taken at Harry's First Holy Communion

Grandson Cian awarded an honour in college.

Launch of Flannery Village

My son Patrick climbed the 32 counties tallest mountains.

Martin McGuiness and his wife Bernie visiting my family home in happier times. Myself and Martin go back a long time and we have always been behind a united Ireland.

Mark Flannery, busy working hard even at a young age.

Patrick with Mary at her daughter's
wedding in the castle in Sligo.

My Two Daughters Christina and Katharina dancing at a
jiving competition in the Talk of Town in Banger Erris.

FLANNERY COUSINS IN THE U.S.A.

Anthony & Winnifred Flannery, parents of nine sons & one daughter.

Anthony Flannery's father was the generation who left Porturlin all those years ago and carried the Flannery name through the USA and achieved so much.

Anthony & Winnifred Flannery, cousins in the USA.

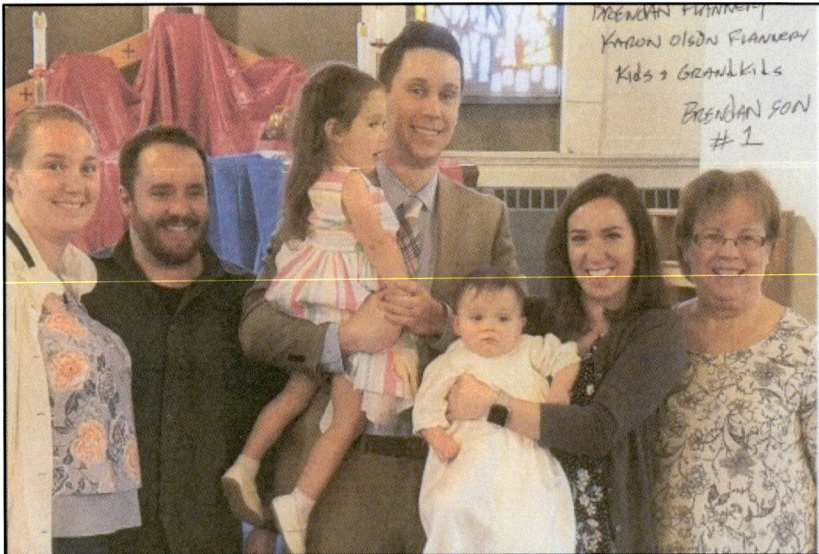

Brendan Flannery & Karen Olson Flannery with kids and
grandkids, cousins in the USA.

Brian & Anne Flannery with kids and grandkids

Brendan & Karen Flannery, cousin living in the USA

Flannery cousins get together in Connecticut, USA.

*Patrick Flannery enjoying a Guinness with his
friend John Connell from USA*

Kareah Flannery, Kathleen Flannery's daughter and grandchild.

Kevin & Sharon
Flannery with sons
Liam & Noel.

Kieran Flannery's kids

Owen Flannery's grandchildren

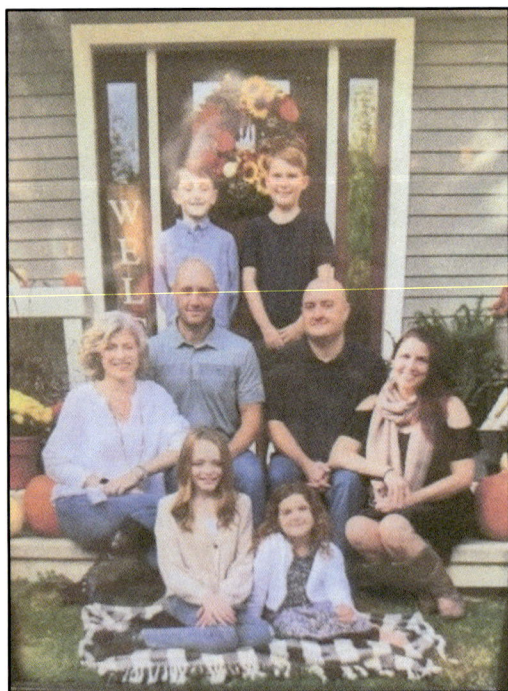

Owen & Dawn Flannery
with sons and
grandchildren

FARMERS JOURNAL
THE VOICE OF IRELAND'S BIGGEST INDUSTRY

IFI
IRISH FERTILIZER INDUSTRIES

Teagasc
AGRICULTURE AND FOOD DEVELOPMENT AUTHORITY

RICHARDSONS FERTILIZERS

DEPARTMENT OF AGRICULTURE FOR NORTHERN IRELAND

Farm Development Awards 1997

This is to certify that

Patrick Flannery

is a Category Winner in the Farm Development Awards 1997

The award is given in recognition of outstanding farm progress from 1993 - 1997

Signed _____

This competition is sponsored by the Irish Farmers' Journal,
Irish Fertilizer Industries, Teagasc and Richardsons Fertilizers,
in association with the Department of Agriculture for Northern Ireland

Bord Iascaigh Mhara,
National Fishery Training Centre,
Greencastle,
Co. Donegal.

Certificate Number BSS 1589

This is to Certify that

Name ....Patrick Flannery............

Address ....Partraun............

............Tawnagh, Co. Mayo............

Date of Birth ....15th April 1953............

has successfully completed a

Basic Sea Survival Course

approved by the

Irish Department of the Marine

held on

Date ....3rd May 1990............

At ....Pollins Swimming Pool............

Derek O'Connor
Instructor in charge of Course

Date of Issue ....3rd May 1990............

(Stamp of N.F.T.C.)

Spar Local Hero
Awards 2003

This certificate has been presented to

Patrick Flannery

in recognition of great personal achievement
and contribution to the welfare and
quality of life of others.

Mobile
Training
Unit

This is to Certify

Mr Patrick Flannery of Partraun, Ballina
Co. Mayo satisfactorily completed the Small Boat
Electrics, Radio, and Safety Course

Senior Instructor ....Tom Kelly............

Instructor ....

Date ....14-5-05............

CERT. NO. 1460.

Launch of first book, 'Don't Give Up' in 2008

Fishing in Porturlin Harbour
& Salmon Driftner Fishermen

The following is an article from Western People, January 2nd 2002

Pullathomas man is new spokesman for salmon driftnet fishermen

Patrick Flannery of Graughill, Pullathomas was recently elected by the salmon driftnet fishermen to represent them as spokesperson for the North West Board area. Here, Patrick writes about the concerns of the fishermen he represents and calls on the government to act with urgency in meeting the needs of the fishermen.

Like many ports along the north west coast of Ireland, Porturlin and Belderrig in County Mayo have provided a good living and healthy lifestyle from the sea for many years. In days gone by, the men fished the sea while the women used the catch to rear their families. This trraditional way of living was handed down from generation to generation.

While good deals for Irish farmers were made and welcomed, the rights of fishermen were sold out and forgotten. Because the salmon stock was seen to be decreasing, the salmon fishermen were given fewer and fewer hours to earn their living. They were paid a fee by the government to cull the seal population. Then the government brought in laws to protect the seals.

From my own experience, I know that for an annual catch of 800 salmon, the seals will get 3 times that many. The government regulations imposed by the Central Fishery Board decreased the salmon fishing time from 5 days and must be protected, so must the rights of the fishermen be protected.

Over the past few years, young fishermen in Porturlin and fishing villages along the north west coast have made significant investment in upgrading their boats to fish salmon, improve and continue a way of life taught to them from the time they were kids. For many, it is the only life they know, or ever will know. With government imposed reductions in days and hours for fishing, the fishermen should be compensated in much the same way the farmers were compensated for forced de-stocking their farms.

The government has forgotten about the fishermen. My belief is that fishermen should have rights the same as farmers, the same as tourism, because the fishermen are so important to our environment and our tourism along these coasts. As chairman of Iorras Domhann Tourism Co-Op in Belmullet, I met with Mr Frank Fahy last Friday in Belmullet as one of several local people involved in tourism and welcomed him to Erris with £100,000 tourism pilot project.

The fishing ports like Porturlin where there are 19 boats fishing 9 months of the year, have to be upgraded to correct years and years of neglect. Safety regulations in fishing ports are contravened because fishermen must row out to their fishing vessels, anchored in the harbour in small little row boats because the piers are not fit to dock their fishing boats. On several occasions, I have brought tourists to Porturlin to go deep sea rod fishing and was delayed 2-3 hours waiting for the tide to allow boats to dock at the pier. This sutuation must be remedied immediately. Porturlin alone would require about £2mllion investment to upgrade the harbour.

I have contacted a spokesperson for Mayo County Council and have been advised that the Council have appointed consulting engineers to prepare a preliminary report for harbour improvements in Porturlin. The report is expected early in 2002. The proposal will probably involve a foreshore licence from the Department of the Marine. It will slo be necessary to carry out a part-ten planning process.

The Council has been in touch with the Department of the Marine on this proposal and assuming that capital monies can be made available next year, the Council would hope to be in a position to seek tenders and proceed with the project next year.

North Western Regional Fisheries Board

Bord Iascaigh Réigiúnach an Iarthuaiscirt

Fisheries Ireland
Our Natural Heritage

27 Apr, 2006

Dear Sir

I refer to your application for a Salmon Drift Net Licence for 2006 and wish to inform you that it has been approved by my Board.

It is proposed to issue licence number D 767 to you.

Before the licence can be issued, it will be necessary for you to comply with the following:-

(a) If your boat is registered under Section 373 of the Merchant Shipping Act, 1894, the registered letters and number must be marked on the boat in accordance with regulations.

OR

(b) The number of the licence to be issued to you (D 767) must be marked on **each bow** with distinct figures of not less than **six inches in length and one inch in breadth**. This number shall be painted directly on to each bow in white oil colour on a black background. *Please note that your boat must be properly numbered before a licence is issued to you.* As soon as you have complied with this requirement, please return the enclosed form together with a remittance for €337.00.

Your boat will be inspected by Board staff during the week commencing 8 May, 2006. You should ensure that it is in port during that week and that it is suitably numbered. Otherwise, it will be assumed that you do not wish to pursue your application for 2006. If everything is in order, the licence will then be issued. Please note **you are not entitled to fish for salmon until the licence has been formally issued to you.**

*All licences must be taken out by **Thursday, 25 May, 2006**. Licences not taken out by that date will be awarded to the next qualified applicant who has applied.*

Yours sincerely

VINCENT ROCHE
Chief Executive Officer

The North Western Regional
Fisheries Board
Ardnaree House
Abbey Street
Ballina
Co. Mayo

Porturlin Fishing Harbour

Glenamoy Angling Club
info@glenamoyangling.com

Salmon fishing

Pullathomas hero honoured in Dublin

Patrick Flannery receiving the SPAR Local Hero Award from Alex Banahan, Marketing Director, SPAR, and Mary Davis, CEO, Special Olympics at the Mansion House, Dublin.

THE SPAR Local Hero Awards 2003, in association with The Irish Sun, culminated in an honours lunch at the Mansion House on Wednesday, 19th November where ten extraordinary Irish citizens were honoured for the invaluable difference they have made, to the lives of others. This very special event was hosted by Ian Dempsey, Today FM and attended by Special Olympics CEO, Mary Davis and Dublin?'s Deputy Lord Mayor, Cllr. Deirdre Heney.

Patrick Flannery from Pullathomas was presented with a €500 travel bursary and framed certificate for the outstanding effect he has had on his local community. Patrick was nominated for this award by his partner Theresa McGrath because without him she herself, her daughter Siobhain and her daughter's boyfriend Anthony wouldn't be with us today.

On the 19th of September, Theresa encouraged Patrick to join her at a fundraising event for a local boy and so Siobhan and Anthony set off in their car, followed by Theresa and Patrick in theirs.

Shortly after leaving their house the skies opened and on a dark and dangerous cliff road both cars were suddenly lifted off the road by flash floods and landslides and moving backwards along the road until Anthony's car perilously dangled on the edge of the road overhanging the cliff.

According to Theresa it was the hand of God, and another movement of earth that shifted the car from the edge. Patrick's car was also surrounded by mud and water, moving in torrents around the car. Patrick forced his way out of the car, went to help Anthony and Siobhan and then as quickly as possible moved everyone to higher ground and to safety.

H s quick thinking and courage saved lives that night.

The following is from a report by Mayo County Council regarding the landslides in Co Mayo. June 29th 2004

Update Report on the Landslides at Dooncarton, Glengad, Barnachuille and Pollathomas, Co Mayo.

Mayo County Council,
Altamont Street
Westport
Co Mayo.

TOBIN Consulting Engineers
Galway & Castlebar
Dundalk & Limerick

DOCUMENT AMENDMENT RECORD

Client	Mayo County Council
Project	North Mayo Landslide
Title	Update Report on the Landslides at Dooncarton, Glengad, Barnachuille and Pollathomais, County Mayo

Project No.		2033	Document Ref:		2033 Landslide Report May '04.doc	
Revision	Purpose / Description	Originated	Checked	Authorised		Date
0	Report issued to Client	PG	MFG	MFG		21/05/04
A	Updated Report issued	MFG	MFG	MFG		10/06/04
B	Revisions	MFG	MFG	MFG		29/06/04

TOBIN CONSULTING ENGINEERS, MARKET SQUARE, CASTLEBAR, COUNTY MAYO

TOBIN
Patrick J. Tobin & Co. Ltd

Report on the Landslides at Dooncarton, Glengad, Barnachuille and Pollathomais, County Mayo

TABLE OF CONTENTS

TOBIN
Patrick J. Tobin & Co. Ltd

Updated Report on the Landslides at Dooncarton, Glengad, Barnachuille and Pollathomais, County Mayo, May 2004.

EXECUTIVE SUMMARY

This updating report on the original submission of October 29th 2003 examines the implications of the latest survey on Dooncarton Mountain and environs, in May 2004, and it assesses the behaviour of the loosened deposits on the slopes of the mountain over the first winter period since the events of September 2003.

TOBIN

INTRODUCTION AND TERMS OF REFERENCE

On the night of September 19th, 2003, intense localised rainfall caused multiple landslides on the slopes of Dooncarton and Barnachuille mountains. The combined effects of floodwater and landslides caused widespread damage to the public road infrastructure, to the old and new graveyards, and to private property.

TOBIN Consulting Engineers, in October 2003, submitted a report assessing the immediate condition of the slopes of the Dooncarton and Barnachuille mountains at Pollathomais, County Mayo, and advising the Council in their response to widespread landslides and floodwater damage.

That Report assessed the risk environment for the public infrastructure, including roads, culverts, bridges, and the graveyard and also residential properties in the immediate aftermath of the event, and it was clear that it would be necessary to keep that assessment under review, initially as the survey information flow progressed, but in the medium term as the loosened peat deposits weathered toward a new equilibrium during the first winter.

It is now timely to review the position as it stood at the time of our report of October 2003, in the light of the considerable remedial works carried out by Mayo County Council and the Office of Public Works in the interim period, and to

- review the risks of further landslides occurring, and the possible consequences of these
- determine the necessary protection and risk mitigation works as matters stand in May 2004
- review the effectiveness of the interim works carried out in the immediate aftermath of the events of September 2003 and review the recommendations on long term protection works and precautionary measures

TOBIN

INSPECTION OF THE LANDSLIDES AT DOONCARTON, GLENGAD AND BARNACUILLE

Inspection Team: Steven Verity, Executive Engineer, Mayo County Council,

        Dan Duggan, Senior Geologist, TOBIN Consulting Engineers,

        Peter Gannon, Senior Technician, TOBIN Consulting

        Engineers,

The Site was visited and surveyed on Thursday 20th May 2004.

Weather Conditions: Good visibility, Clear and sunny with light showers and

        blustery winds.

Ground Conditions: Very Dry as a result of two to three weeks of antecedent fine

        weather

AREA A:

This area, indicated on Drg No 2033 – 1007 of the original report, includes Property No.'s: 24, 25, 26, 27, 28, 29, 30, 31, 32, 33, 34, 35, 36, 37, 38, 39, 40, 41, 42, 43, 44, 45, 46. Having surveyed the position related to the various clusters of homes in the area, the following represents our updated assessment of the conditions in May 2004.

Property No. 43 & 39:

Originally these properties were included in the High Risk Zone due to the discovery of tension cracks upgradient towards the end of our initial survey in September 2003. The recommended berm has since been reconstructed in this area, and due to the fact that the land slope is not as steep over these particular properties, and recognising that the tension cracks in this area have shown little activity over the intervening months, we would recommend that these properties be reduced in classification to Medium Risk.

Property No. 38 & 37:

From our most recent inspection we have discovered that there is still a large area of peat that has the potential to cause damage to these properties. Also, there are loose boulders which

have emerged as weathering has taken place in the scarred surface, that now have the potential to move and cause damage. This is an area of the mountain, which has a very steep slope (approximately 1/1), with a short travel distance to these properties, as shown on the photographs below. These properties will continue to require the construction of the Kinetic Barrier Fence to the rear, so as to reduce the risk associated with the current state of the slopes. Once the fence is constructed, it will be possible to reclassify these properties from High Risk to Medium Risk. Substantial improvement works have been carried out by Mayo County Council and the Office of Public Works (OPW) to the existing drainage network in this area. The recent addition of the box culvert to the lower side of Property No. 37 and the upgrading and improvement works to the roadside drainage network along the upper Glengad Road (LT12025) will assist with future flood flow patterns in this area. The new drainage system constructed behind the reinforced berm, directing flows to existing drains and culverts will also assist, should there be another rainfall event of the same order of magnitude.

Plate No. 1   Loose Material over Property No. 38 & No.37

Plate No. 2   16.8m x 8.5m x 0.85m Detached Block over Property 38 & 37

Plate No. 3   Loose Rock in the surface Scar over Properties 38 & 37

Property No. 32 & 31:

To the rear of Property No. 32, the original berm has been reconstructed and reinforced. The area directly behind this property is higher that the surrounding lands, and with the addition of a second berm directly to the rear of Property No. 32, and the improvement works to the drainage network, we consider that even without the addition of the Kinetic Barrier Fence in this area, the works carried out to date will be sufficient to reduce the classification of this property from High Risk to Medium Risk at this time.

Plate No. 4   New Berm to rear of Property No. 32 and Reinforced Berm over

Property No. 31:

This property is located beside the main drainage channel from the catchment basin of Area A1. Mayo County Council are at this time reconstructing the culvert serving this subcatchment and have reinforced the sides of this drainage channel. Further works are to be carried out in this area in relation to the drainage issues, but with the quality of the reconstructed berm to the rear of this property, we are of the opinion that this property can be reduced in classification from High to Medium risk once all works are completed in this area.

Property No.'s: 24, 25, 26, 27, 28, 29, 30, 31, 33, 34, 35, 36, 40, 41, 42, 44, 45, 46

With the improvement works to the drainage network and the reconstruction of the protection berm along with upgraded roadside drainage, these properties are now at a much reduced risk of damage from a similar event.

AREA A1

This area continues to weather and the larger aggregations of peat are breaking down as we anticipated. The larger blocks are detaching and breaking down over the scar surface (see

Plate No. 4 & 5). As the material from this area will eventually end up in the basin below, we feel that this area is generally behaving as we had previously expected and described in our report of October 2003.

Plate No. 5   *Detached Blocks in Area A1 breaking down over scarred surface*

Plate No. 6:   Detached Blocks sliding towards Basin Area Below

TOBIN

AREA E

Includes Property No.'s 7, 11, 12, 13, 14, 15, 16, 17, 18, 19, 20

This landslide area is the second most active zone of the whole area, with large blocks detaching and moving / sliding downslope up to distances of nearly 150m. While the majority of properties in this area are outside and away from any threat from this material, Property No. 12 still remains at risk. Some improvement works have been carried out to the old berm in this area and drainage network has been improved but further works will be required to bring this property from High to Medium risk. The addition of a new berm to defect flow and materials away from property 12 will be required. The new berm will be the initial point of impact should any material overtop the intermediate ledge. This measure will reduce the risk associated with property No. 12 from high to medium.

For properties No.'s 13 to 21 inclusive, our report of October 2003 required that a new berm be constructed and also indicated that drainage improvements would be required. Mayo County Council and the OPW have since reinstated the existing berm to a satisfactory standard and have improved the drainage network in this area. These works have restored the drainage efficiency of this area and with the improved drainage network along the main road this will reduce risk levels to low level.

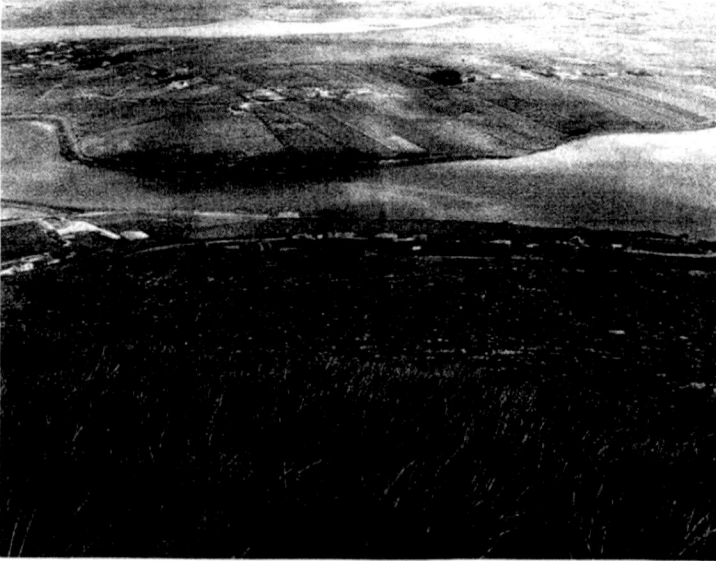

Plate No. 7   Property No. 12 shown in relation to Berm at the top road in Barnacuille

AREA B

Includes Property No.'s 0, 1, 2, 3, 4, 5, 6, 8, 9, 10,

Property No. 0 – The Graveyard:

The area between S2 & S3 is very wet due to springs and groundwater in the saddle area over these two landslide areas. This water has the effect of lubricating the disturbed material and is causing further detachment in this area. The short travel distance to the reconstructed berm and the steep downslope gradient along with the second steep slope below mean that the construction of the Kinetic Fence will continue to be required to protect the graveyard.

Property No. 2 & 3:

Mayo County Council and the OPW have carried out a lot of improvement works to the roadside drainage network and the existing drainage channels and gullies. The improved berm to the rear of properties no. 1 & 2 plus the improved roadside drainage has reduced the risk to these properties.

Plate No. 8   Reinforced berm shown in relation to Property No. 3, Property No. 1
Not visible from Top Slope

Property No. 5:

The same criteria exist for Property No. 5 as at landslide areas S2 & S3 except for the fact that there are no springs or groundwater lubricating this area where the disturbed material rests at S12 & S13. The reconstructed single berm will not be sufficient to protect this property, so the addition of the Kinetic Barrier Fence to the rear of this property continues to be required.

Property No. 8, 9, 10:

Properties 9 and 10 are currently unoccupied, and the berm improvement works upslope have reduced their risk status from High to Medium, as is the case with Property No. 8.

Plate No. 9   Reinforced berm Shown in Relation to Property No. 5

Property No.'s 3 & 4:

The addition of the new berm along the front of Property No. 5 will add the protection required for the two properties below (Property No.'s 3 & 4). This along with the drainage improvements and the channel lining along the sides of the top road will reduce the risks in this area.

Property No. 6:

Property No. 6 was subjected to overtopping of the existing drainage system during the event on September 19th 2003, but with the improved protection works completed upslope by the reconstruction of the berm and the improved roadside drainage along the LT52431 (Barnacuille Road) the risk to this property will be reduced significantly.

TOBIN

DRAINAGE WORKS:

Mayo County Council and the Office of Public Works have carried out a series of remedial works to the drainage network along the main road (LP1202), the Glengad Road (LT12025) and the Barnacuille Road (LT52431). The retaining wall at the graveyard has been reconstructed and extended and the banks of the drain have been reinforced where required. The complete roadside drainage network has been upgraded with roadside drainage channels opened and discharge channels to the sea have been reinstated and cleaned. This work along with the improvement works upgradient on the slopes to the drainage network will direct the future flows to the improved drainage networks below.

Flannery - Politics and Local Elections

Flannery to stand for Erris Sinn Fein in council elections
Article printed in Western Peope, 3rd September 2003

The Belmullet sons of Erris Sinn Fein Cumman held a meeting in McGuire's Pub, Pullathomas on Tuesday August 26th. The purpose of the meeting was to nominate a candidate to stand in the next council election in May 2004. A motion was proposed that Patrick Flannery of Flannery Village be nominated to go forward. The motion was seconded and strongly supported by unanimous decision.

In his acceptance speech, Patrick talked about the raw deal given to the fishermen, that they were sold out by the government. He has been a vocal spokesman for the North West Driftnet Fishermen for the past two years, a voluntary position to make the concerns of the fishermen widely known. Mr Flannery mentioned the poor quality of the road from Erris to Caslebar (especially bad for those who are travelling urgently to Mayo General Hospital, such as heavily pregnant expectant mothers, some of whom were forced to give birth on the roadside.) In the past, politicians who came into Erris along that same bad road took votes away and failed the Erris people. Patrick spoke of the often-promised but never delivered X-Ray unit for Belmullet Community Hospital. He mentioned funds that had been raised both at home and abroad for this effort and still no X-Ray unit in Erris.

Patrick Flannery has been a promoter of tourism in Erris for many years and has built a successful holiday village and knitwear faxctory which attracts visitors from all over the world. Patrick voiced the concerns of the local population over the proposed Corrib Gas development, to ensure that the project, if it goes ahead, will be done with the utmost respect and safety for the environment and the people of Erris. In a recent meeting with Shell Mayo Area Manager, Mr Mark Carrigy and

Mr John Cronin, Patrick again stressed his continuing concern with environmental and economic issues. Mr Carrigy assured Patrick and the people of Erris that he will keep them updated on plans and progress of the gas project.

Patrick says Sinn Fein won't make promises they can't keep, and won't sell the rights of the people or their country.

Frequent visitor to Flannery Village and special guest on the night was **Martin McGuinness, MP**. Martin spoke to the over 150 people present and encouraged the continued organisation of Sinn Fein in Erris. He reminded all present that Sinn Fein is the third largest and fastest growing political party in Ireland, as well as the ONLY all-Ireland party. Martin is a long time personal friend of Patrick Flannery and was happy to endorse Patrick's nomination for candidacy in the upcoming council election. During his recent stay Mr McGuinness was given a guided tour of SELC Ireland Limited by owner and Mayo Man of the Year, Mr Sean Noone. Also in Belmullet, Martin was warmly welcomed by staff at the offices of Udaras Na Gaeltachta. One of the highlights of his visit was a trip to the Inishkea Islands courtesy of the Belmullet Sub Aqua Club.

Patrick wishes to sincerely thank all the people of Erris who made Mr McGuinness feel so welcome. Special thanks was due to the McGuire family of Pullathomas for the food provided for everyone on the night.

Mr Martin McGuinness MP pictured in Erris last week with Patrick Flannery, who has been selected as the Sinn Fein candidate in the next year's elections to Mayo County Council.

Martin McGuinness informed 'Open Agenda' that he tries to be a regular visitor to Erris whenever the Northern negotiations allow. During his latest visit, he stayed in the Pullathomas area. *"I love the west of Ireland but this part of Mayo is absolutely beautiful,"* he said.

* HE MOVES THROUGH THE FAIR..... Martin McGuinness joined the throngs at Belmullet Fair last week. Photo- Ken Wright.

* Patrick Flannery from Bangor Erris will be a Sinn Fein candidate in the next County Council elections. Photo-Ken Wright

MARTIN
McGUINNESS 1

HELP ELECT YOUR PRESIDENT

Martin was born in Derry in 1950, one of seven children. He has been married to Bernie for 37 years. They have four children – Grainne, Fionnuala, Fiachra and Emmet – and five grandchildren. He is a keen fisherman and poet. He is an avid sports fan and in particular follows Derry GAA and Derry City FC.

Join Martin's Campaign Team

26 Counties: Text MARTIN2011 with your NAME and ADDRESS to 51444
6 Counties: Text MARTIN2011 with your NAME and ADDRESS to 60060

Donate to Martin's Campaign

Visit us on www.thepeoplespresident.ie

Contact the Campaign

Web: www.thepeoplespresident.ie
Email: admin@thepeoplespresident.ie
Tweet: @martin4prez2011
Facebook: www.facebook.com/Martin4President

This literature is available as gaeilge. If you would like a copy please contact Martin's campaign team at admin@thepeoplespresident.ie

ELECTION DAY: 27th OCTOBER

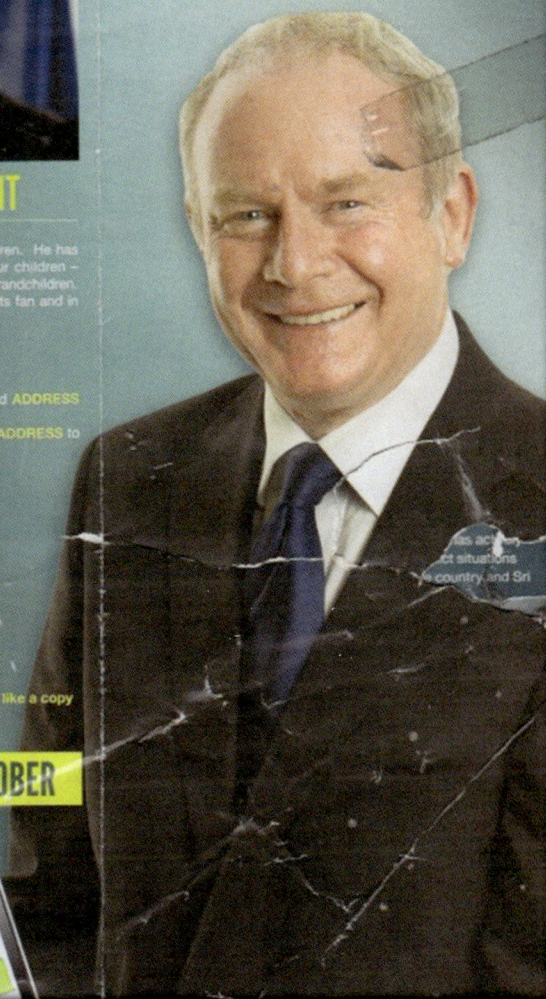

MARTIN'S POLITICAL JOURNEY

Derry Republican

Martin's political journey began on the streets of Derry in the late 1960s when he joined the marches for Civil Rights. From his early days he has been guided by the vision of reuniting our country. He joined the IRA in the 1970s. He was present on Bloody Sunday when 14 of his fellow citizens of Derry were murdered by the British Army.

Peace Negotiator

In the late 1980s and early 1990s, Martin worked alongside John Hume, Albert Reynolds, Gerry Adams and others in bringing about the IRA ceasefire and the development of the peace process. He was elected to the peace negotiations in 1996 and was appointed the Sinn Féin Chief Negotiator in the talks which led to the Good Friday Agreement.

Education Minister

Martin became Education Minister in 1999 and put equality for all children at the heart of his education policy. He took the landmark decision to end the socially divisive system of academic segregation, the '11 plus', while promoting Irish-medium and integrated education. As Minister he prioritised and increased funding for children with special needs and those from socially disadvantaged communities.

Deputy First Minister

In 2007 Martin became the North's deputy First Minister alongside Ian Paisley, a position he currently holds alongside the new DUP leader, Peter Robinson. His approach on the Executive and the All-Ireland Ministerial Council has been one of partnership, equality and inclusion and he has helped demonstrate that politics can and do work for all in our society.

MARTIN McGUINNESS

Martin McGuinness has been an extremely influential person in Irish politics for many years and a critical figure in developing and sustaining the Peace Process. He has a deep love of Ireland and a vision of where Ireland as a nation needs to go.

As deputy First Minister in the North, Martin has shown leadership in working closely and successfully with the representatives of unionism. He has dedicated himself to a genuine national reconciliation and the unity of our people.

Martin is now a key figure on the international stage.

He has a considerable international reputation as a peacemaker and has actively assisted in the search for peace in other conflict situations.

And, as deputy First Minister, he has built international relations and worked successfully to attract major economic investment to the North.

The next President will have to give leadership to the Irish people through one of the most difficult periods in our history. The President will lead the Irish nation as we mark the centenary of the 1916 Rising and must also lead a debate on our country's future.

As Uachtarán na hÉireann, Martin McGuinness will work for the reunification of Ireland. He will stand up for Ireland. He will be a President for all the people.

UACHTARÁN NA nDAOINE

- Is í na Mháirtín éirinn níos fearr agus níos féaráilte, áit a mbeidh pobal agus sochaí níos tábhachtaigh ná rathúnas eacnamaíoch.
- Má thoghtar é mar Uachtarán ní ghlacfaidh sé ach an meán pha.
- Bainfidh sé úsáid as an Uachtaránacht chun aitheantas a thabhairt do pháirteachas saoránach, ina measc, iad siúd a bhfuil a gcuid oibre ina gcuid pobail riachtanach chun sochaí láidir sláintiúil a chothú.
- Dhéanfaidh Máirtín Áras an Uachtaráin fáilteach do gach roinn de shochaí na hÉireann, go háirithe iad siúd a bhí imeallaithe go dtí seo.
- Beidh Máirtín ina Uachtarán ag iomlán, diaspóra na hÉireann san áireamh.

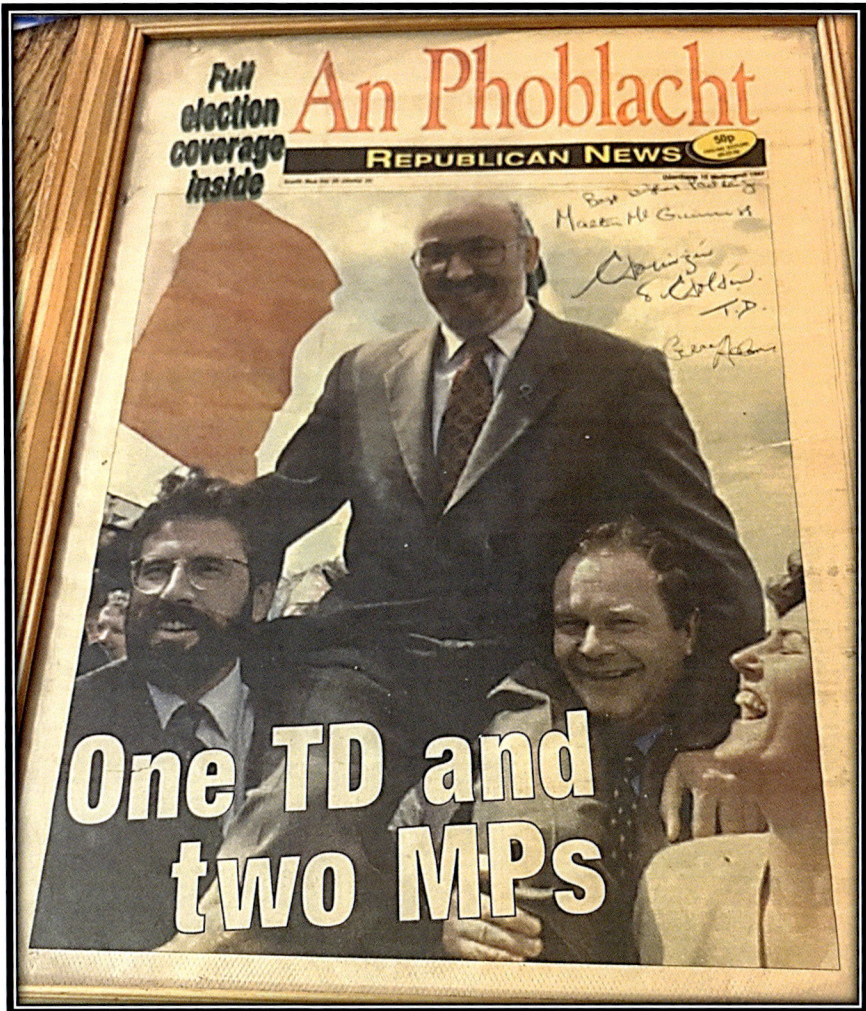

'Martin McGuinness was not a terrorist, Martin McGuinness was a freedom fighter'

POBLACHT NA H EIREANN.

THE PROVISIONAL GOVERNMENT
OF THE

IRISH REPUBLIC
TO THE PEOPLE OF IRELAND.

IRISHMEN AND IRISHWOMEN: In the name of God and the dead generations from which she receives her old tradition of nationhood, Ireland, through us, summons her children to her flag and strikes for her freedom.

Having organised and trained her manhood through her secret revolutionary organisation, the Irish Republican Brotherhood, and through her open military organisations, the Irish Volunteers and the Irish Citizen Army, having patiently perfected her discipline, having resolutely waited for the right moment to reveal itself, she now seizes that moment, and, supported by her exiled children in America and by gallant allies in Europe, but relying in the first on her own strength, she strikes in full confidence of victory.

We declare the right of the people of Ireland to the ownership of Ireland, and to the unfettered control of Irish destinies, to be sovereign and indefeasible. The long usurpation of that right by a foreign people and government has not extinguished the right, nor can it ever be extinguished except by the destruction of the Irish people. In every generation the Irish people have asserted their right to national freedom and sovereignty; six times during the past three hundred years they have asserted it in arms. Standing on that fundamental right and again asserting it in arms in the face of the world, we hereby proclaim the Irish Republic as a Sovereign Independent State, and we pledge our lives and the lives of our comrades in arms to the cause of its freedom, of its welfare, and of its exaltation among the nations.

The Irish Republic is entitled to, and hereby claims, the allegiance of every Irishman and Irishwoman. The Republic guarantees religious and civil liberty, equal rights and equal opportunities to all its citizens, and declares its resolve to pursue the happiness and prosperity of the whole nation and of all its parts, cherishing all the children of the nation equally, and oblivious of the differences carefully fostered by an alien government, which has divided a minority from the majority in the past.

Until our arms have brought the opportune moment for the establishment of a permanent National Government, representative of the whole people of Ireland and elected by the suffrages of all her men and women, the provisional Government, hereby constituted, will administer the civil and military affairs of the Republic in trust for the people.

We place the cause of the Irish Republic under the protection of the Most High God, Whose blessing we invoke upon our arms, and we pray that no one who serves that cause will dishonour it by cowardice, inhumanity, or rapine. In this supreme hour the Irish nation must, by its valour and discipline and by the readiness of its children to sacrifice themselves for the common good, prove itself worthy of the august destiny to which it is called.

Signed on Behalf of the Provisional Government.

THOMAS J. CLARKE.

SEAN Mac DIARMADA.   THOMAS MacDONAGH.
P. H. PEARSE.   EAMONN CEANNT.
JAMES CONNOLLY.   JOSEPH PLUNKETT.

Irish Northern Aid Committee
Testimonial Dinner

363 Seventh Avenue • Suite 405 • New York, NY 10001 •
noraid1971@aol.com • www.inac.org

A Chara,

On Saturday, January 25, 2003 the Irish Northern Aid Committee will hold its 32nd annual Testimonial Dinner Dance at the South Gate Hotel.
We will be honoring four people who have, and will continue to support a free and United Ireland. Our honorees this year are Eamon Meehan. Eamon has been in prison in 5 different Countries over his lifetime fighting for a United Ireland. Noreen McDonald from Galway, Malachy McDonald from Portadown both in Noraid for the past thirty years and our own Liam O'Keefe who will be getting the Bob McCann award for dedicating thirty years to The Irish People Paper.

Kevin and Tom Smith will be our entertainment this year along with the New York City Police Departments Emerald Society Bag Pipers

Tickets for this event are $100.00 per person and $1000.00 a table. We will also be publishing our Testimonial Journal which will offer three types of ads. A gold page for $200.00, a full White page for $150.00 and half page for $75.00. Enclosed is some Journal contracts, which can be duplicated and distributed to friends and supporters.

The events of the past month, where the British Government once again has suspended the Assembly to placate David Trimble will only give momentum to those who are opposed to the Good Friday Agreement. The raid on the Sinn Fein Office while despicable, and the arrest of four people including Dennis Donaldson on trumped up spying accusation is further proof that the British Government is unwilling to act impartially

It is obvious that this is a crucial time in Irish history and as Gerry Adams has stated on numerous occasions we all have a role to play in bring about peace with justice in the North of Ireland. I hope and trust that the suffering people in Ireland can count on your support.

Is mise le meas,

Paddy Dolan
Dinner Chair

- 140 -

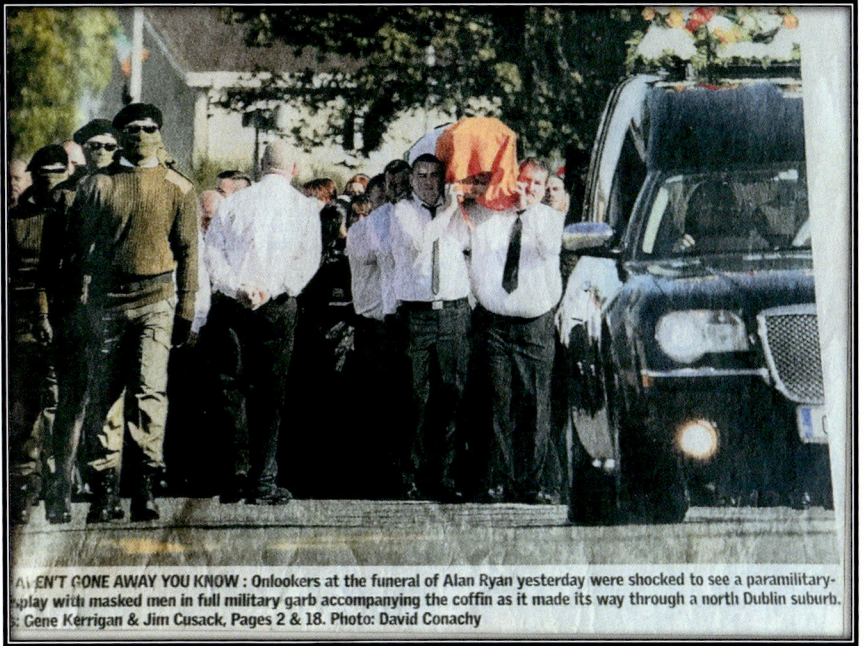

AVEN'T GONE AWAY YOU KNOW : Onlookers at the funeral of Alan Ryan yesterday were shocked to see a paramilitary-
display with masked men in full military garb accompanying the coffin as it made its way through a north Dublin suburb.
: Gene Kerrigan & Jim Cusack, Pages 2 & 18. Photo: David Conachy

Republican Roll of Honour 20[...]

2011 annual
dublin volunteers
dinner dance

A night of
Celebration and
Remembrance

bhliantúil 2011
átha cliath
oibrithe deonacha
damhsa dinnéar

8pm Saturday 26th November
Gresham Hotel, O'Connell Street
» Chaired by Seán Crowe TD   » Guest speaker: Rita O'Hare

SPECIAL HONOUREE:
ROSE DUGDALE

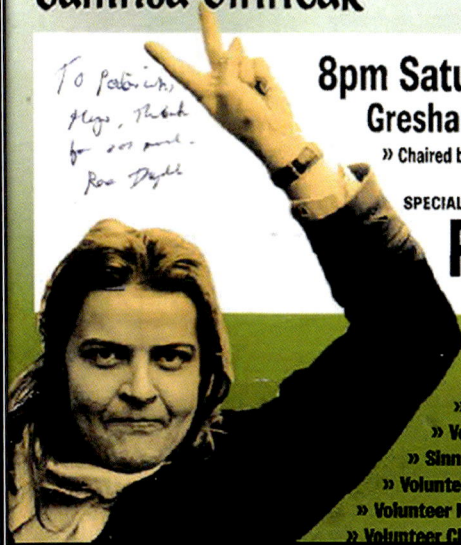

REMEMBERING WITH PRIDE
OUR FALLEN COMRADES:
» Volunteer Tom Smith 17th March 1975
» Volunteer Patrick Cannon 17th July 1976
» Sinn Féin member Jeff McKenna 8th November 1982
» Volunteer Colm Daltún 15th January 1983
» Volunteer Mick Timothy 26th January 1985
» Volunteer Christy Harford 5th May 1992

REMEMBERING WITH PRIDE OUR FALLEN COMRADES

Volunteer Tom Smith
17th March 1975

Volunteer Patrick Cannon
17th July 1976

Sinn Féin member Jeff McKenna
8th November 1982

Volunteer Colm Daltún
15th January 1983

Volunteer Mick Timothy
26th January 1985

Volunteer Christy Harford
5th May 1992

Volunteer Martin Doherty
21st May 1994

Comhgháirdeas do Rose Dugdale ar do oíche speisialta ó fhoireann Shinn Féin Teach Laighean

Gerry Adams TD, Mary Lou McDonald TD, Pearse Doherty TD, Aengus O'Snodaigh TD, Caoimhghín Ó Caoláin TD, Martin Ferris TD, Dessie Ellis TD, Séan Crowe TD, Peadar Toibín TD, Sandra McLelland TD, Padraig MacLochlainn TD, Brian Stanley TD, Jonathan O'Brien TD, Michael Colreavy TD, Senator Trevor O'Clochartaigh, Senator Kathryn Reilly, Senator David Cullinane and all the Sinn Féin Party Political Staff at Leinster House also, who wish you all the very best now and for the future.

Congratulations to Rose Dugdale on her special night, from the Sinn Féin Leinster House Team

SEAN McNEELA
BALLYCROY, MAYO.
Died on Hunger Strike
Arbour Hill, Dublin.
April, 1940.

MICHAEL GAUGHAN
BALLINA, MAYO.
Died on Hunger Strike
Parkhurst Prison
June, 1974.

IRISH AMERICA
and the
ULSTER CONFLICT
1968 - 1995

President of America Bill Clinton
and John Hume during the conflict
Northern Ireland

Email DeValaria (Eamon O'Creve)

Éamon de Valera was elected president by the Dail President
from 1919 until early 1922.
He was Taoiseach from 1932 to 1948, from 1951 to 1954 and
from 1957 to 1973
He was president from June 1959 to June 1973
He as born in New York, USA and came to Ireland when he
was two years of age
He returned there in 1919 as president of the Dáil -
Independent Ireland and left at Christmas 1920. As he had
escaped from Lincoln Prison prior to that he had to be
smuggled into the USA and back to Ireland.
He returned to the USA in December 1927 returning in
February 1928
He also spent 6 months in the USA in 1929 collecting money
for the founding of the Irish Press
He visited the USA in 1948 as part of a worldwide anti
partition campaign.
In 1963 he was in Washington for the funeral of John F
Kennedy.
And finally, he went on a State Visit to the USA in 1964
visiting President Johnson and addressing a joint session of
the US Congress
Éamon de Valera did not found Sinn Féin. Sinn Féin was
founded by Arthur Griffith. Éamon de Valera was president of
Sinn Féin from 1917 to 1926
He founded Fianna Fáil in 1926

He wrote many letters many of which are available in the
archives in University College Dublin and some of the most
interesting of which were published in Diarmuid Ferriter's book
Judging Dev.

There is also a great book in which many of the statements he
made and speeches he gave are printed called "Speeches
and Statements by Éamon de Valera edited by Maurice
Moynihan.

I hope this is of use to you.

Éamon

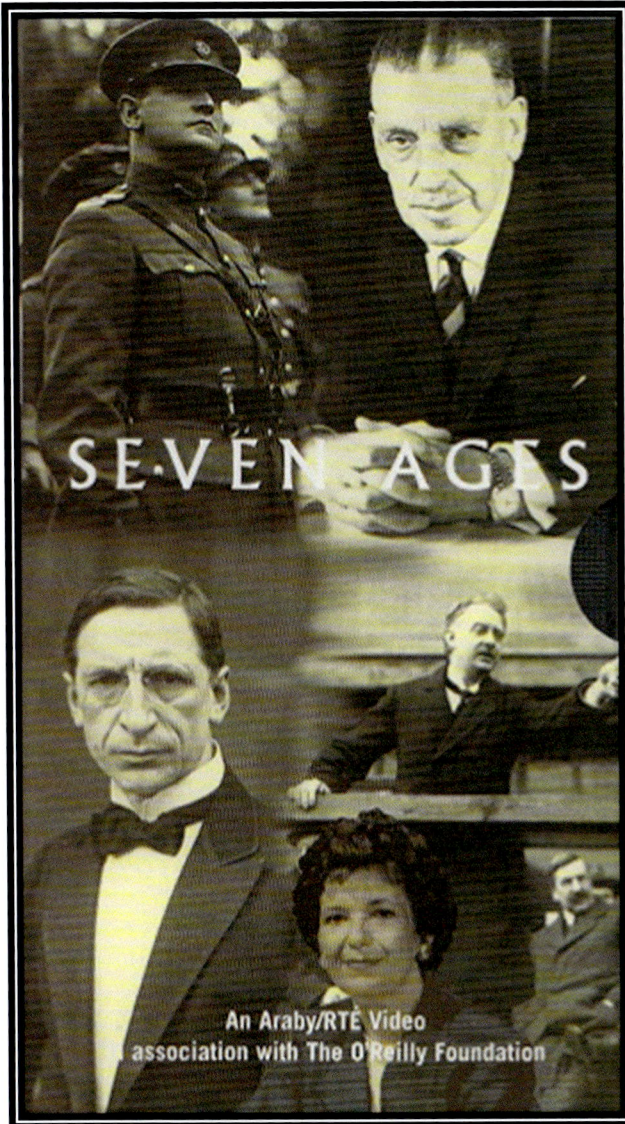

SEVEN AGES

An Araby/RTÉ Video
association with The O'Reilly Foundation

History News Headlines from 'The Western People'

AWFUL SHIPPING DISASTER

LOSS OF TITANIC WITH OVER 1,200 SOULS

THE LOST TITANIC

STORY OF AN APPARITION

TITANIC DISASTER GREAT LOSS OF LIFE
EVENING NEWS

The Titanic Disaster – Lahardane Victim

ONE of the saddest sights ever witnessed in the West of Ireland was the "waking" of the five young girls and a young man from a village near Lahardane that went down with the ill fated Titanic. They were all from the same village, and when the first news of the appalling catastrophe reached their friends the whole community was plunged into unutterable grief. They cherished for a time a remote hope that they were saved, but when the dread news of their terrible fate arrived a feeling of excruciating anguish took its place. For two nights and two days "wakes" were held. The photo of each victim was placed on the bed on which they had slept before leaving home and kindred. The beds were covered with snow white quilts, and numbers of candles were lighted around. The wailing and moaning of the people was most distressing and would almost draw a tear from a stone. The name of the young man that was drowned was John Bourke and in his case his loss is rendered all the sadder by the fact that his young wife went down with him to a watery grave. A strange connection with the Titanic affair. He states that at the time of the disaster he saw his brother in the attitude of shaving himself in his own house.

NORA FLEMING Age 24. Lost at sea. Ticket No: 364859. Bound for New York

PAT CANAVAN Age 21. Lost at sea. Ticket No: 364858. Bound for Philadelphia

MARY MANGAN Age 32. Lost at sea. Ticket No: 364850. Bound for Chicago

JOHN BOURKE - Age 42. Lost at sea. Ticket No: 364849. Bound for Chicago
MARY BOURKE - Age 40. Lost at sea. Ticket No: 364548. Bound for Chicago

ANNIE KATE KELLY Age 20. SURVIVED ON BOAT 16. Ticket No: 9234. Bound for Chicago

CATHERINE McGOWAN Age 42. Lost at sea. Ticket No: 9232. Bound for Chicago

CATHERINE BOURKE Age 32. Lost at sea. Ticket No: 364849. Bound for Chicago

BRIDGET DONOHUE Age 21. Lost at sea. Ticket No: 364856. Bound for Chicago

JAMES FLYNN Age 28. Lost at sea. Ticket No: 364851. Bound for New York

DELIA MAHON Age 20. Lost at sea. Ticket No: 330924. Bound for New York

MARY CANAVAN Age 22. Lost at sea. Ticket No: 364846. Bound for New York

HAIL TO THE VICTORS

MAYO TAKE THEIR THIRD ALL-IRELAND
Meath Were Barely in the Picture

people Special report by
'NLOOKER'

ward was in possession
nal whistle sounded at
on Sunday and the thou
eath supporters did not
had hit them. Yet, for
old hard facts had to be
had won their third All-
and the second one in
creating a new record for
truly a great victory – a
h confounded the pro-
cs, who had openly pro-
ath win a victory which
h of the honour of bring
to New York and which
all manner of fluke or
y abounding luck.
for the 78,201 people in
as rather disappointing
o entered Croke Park
ne could have visualised
ded affair. Even the most
Meath supporter will
act – that the Mayo team
beaten the pick of two
selections of the same
mpant were they last
in short was the full
game and while it may
a plaintive cry from the
caused great jubilation
orters of the western
ers who had turned up
tands to give them that
which the team respond-
ous accent.

SIC

yo viewpoint the out-
game was indeed very
at as football goes it was
m being a classic All-
e first place, there was
he needle element in it
his that caused over-
some passages of the
wever, could not be put
ult of the western side,
y hit hard on occasions,
only team to try and
lay and give the atten-
ing to enthuse about.
vas the only period that
t of good football when
ed by a strong breeze
urn defence into attack
rances. It was mainly
s that the Royal County
coreboard fairly even,
d the better of the
fully deserved their
me. On the turnover,
he breeze, Mayo took
zal and with Meath
ery trick in the bag to
nward march, play
y and very lifeless at

WINNERS

ictory for Mayo would
een an accurate meas-
eir superiority," this
nt from a neutral sup-
ing the pitch and on
merit of victory be
will deny that they
en points better team
I thought one hates to
point, we must say
dered chances which
rily have brought
of 16 wides on Mayo's
o of the game and it
stimation on my part
of those wides should
. In contrast, Meath
des for the first hour,
cannot detract from
for brilliant is the
scribe their display
n Wynne in goal to
all, pulled his weight

and moved with the precision of a
well-oiled machine. Settling down
after Langan scored the first goal,
they beat their opponents in speed,
anticipation and fielding and rarely,
not even in the first half did they
seem to be any way rattled or unsure.
They had the measure of the Meath
men and after the first quarter never
gave their supporters anything to
worry about. They were the real
champions on Sunday and their win,
such as it was, was ample compensa-
tion for the four defeats they suffered
in the past at the hands of the same
team.

ANXIOUS MOMENTS

With such superiority Meath had
many anxious moments during the
game and certainly Lady Luck played
a big part in lightening their defeat.
They were extremely lucky on one
occasion when M. Flanagan, after
receiving from Langan, was just tack-
led at the right moment and was only
inches wide. On another occasion
their goalkeeper, K. Smyth, literally
lay on the ball and was very lucky in
the sense that the referee did not
penalise him. The opinion was
expressed by many that he should
have awarded a penalty to Mayo; but
since the new rules safeguarding
goalkeepers came into force the inter-
pretation of infringements inside the
parallelogram has become more difficult and W. Delaney could be excused
on that occasion. Apart from the
above mentioned passages, the Meath
posts were always in danger and it
was only the indifferent shooting of
the Mayo forwards and not due to any
good defensive play on their own part
that saved them from a more igno-
minious defeat.

LANGAN'S GOAL – A TONIC

With three points of a lead in the
first eight minutes it looked as if the
men from the Royal County were
going to have a successful run but
Langan's goal in the tenth minute was
the signal cry for Mayo to come forward. The score itself is best
described as artistic and it was only

an artist like Langan that could have
secured such a score. Getting possession about 30 yards out, he soloed,
rounded two Meath backs, and shot
from around the 25 yards mark
straight to the corner of the net.
Smyth could not have been blamed for
letting it through, as it was of such a
nature that hardly any goalie would
have saved it. But it was the real tonic
for Mayo and it was from this on they
soared to greater heights. Shortly
afterwards came points from Carney
and Mongey and J. Gilvarry wound
up the first half with a brilliant
opportunist goal.

MIDFIELD SUPREMACY

It is not hard to lay the finger on the
secret of Mayo's success, for their
chief strong point was an all-round
superiority at centrefield. Mongey
and McAndrew struck up a very
happy partnership in this sector and
completely outshone Taaffe and
Connell. To Mongey we must give the
greatest of credit because for the
greater part of the game he was playing under a severe handicap. The
ankle injury which he sustained during the replayed semi-final with
Kerry was again tapped, but this did
not deter him in any way. Through
sheer determination he played on and
later switched places with Carney. He

was far too wily for his opposite number, Taaffe, and must have given one
of his best displays to date. His partner, McAndrew, who after his display
against Kerry was one of the most
maligned players on the side, certainly wiped the smirk off his critic's
faces with his fine performance. He
fielded splendidly, and at times sur-
passing the form which has won him
acclaim in the past, he gave Connell
little scope and kept an endless
stroam of balls streaming goalwards.

QUINLAN AND DIXON WERE GREAT

P. Quinlan, at left-half back, wound
up his football career with a dynamic
display. I have watched this player
since he first entered the ranks back
in 1946 but never was he more effec-
tive than on Sunday last. His task of
marking Meath's danger man was an
unenviable assignment but this he
did in a way that only great players
can. He was simply outstanding and
policed Byrne to such an effort that
the Meath player's presence on the
team was of no benefit whatsoever. It
was really a great climax to a brilliant
career. Dixon, at centre-half back,
played as one inspired. Although
McDonnell got the upper hand for the
first quarter, once Dixon got his meas-

ure his sallies into the goalmouth
were very rare. He was always
dependable and his clearances before
his retiral in the second half were
superb. To counter this Meath
switched B. Smyth to the 40 kept
mark after the interval but he found
the same barrier ever present and the
change resulted in being of no avail.
Stainton on the other wing, played
his typical hard tackling game and
the outcome between himself and the
peerless, P. Meegan, was very keen.
Foremost in the full back line was
Flanagan, playing the game of
Captain Courageous throughout. His
presence was best felt in the first half,
when his well-timed clearances
stemmed the Meath attack and
throughout he inspired and made it.
Smyth, and later McDonnell, look
very small. Prendergast got little to
do but was always there when needed.
He certainly endorsed the right to the
title of the best full back in Ireland, as
after witnessing P. O'Brien's display
there is little room for his claim to
that title. Forde had his hands full in
marking McDermott who succeeded
in scoring two points in the first half.
This, I thought, was no fault on
Forde's part as Meath were working
to a well-timed passing plan, which
was very difficult to intercept.
However, in the second half he kept
him in good check and when
McDermott went into the half-for-
ward line in the second half, Forde
was quick to follow up. Wynne kept a
charmed goal for the full hour and
whenever called upon to clear he did
so in fine fashion.

CARNEY – THE INSPIRATION

"Carney made all the difference".
This statement was in the mouth of

every spectator leaving
have no hesitation in r
the best player on vie
was not at his best in th
kicking, he compensate
a terrific hour's footba
he been seen in better
can well be termed th
chief of Meath's downf
Indian sign on Kelly an
never relaxed his grip fo
was seen at his best in t
when he came to midfi
Mongey and kept the M
the offensive, which c
until the final whistle. C
the league final last Au
supporters were justifie
ing, "If we had Carn
would have won." Flan
Mulderrig, found Heery
crack but his well-place
first half, from about
paved the way for Mayo
Irwin was well held up
the Meath man's retira
the game, as a result
O'Brien was brought fo
vacated half-back posit
coming on as a sub. In O
easier meat and settle
favourable game throug
forward line of Langa
and Gilvarry beat their
session eight out of eve
Though Flanagan's
McConnell had a good g
no answer to the speed
man, who was in hard l
have repeated his perfor
goals. As has already bee
Langan's goal was ra
from the book and this
his clever distribution
made his display outs
round. Whoever said tha
was nearing the end o
made an awful big mis
Joko we witnessed on Su
same player who won h
times on the Connaugh
goal was a well maneuve
one that got Mayo in a
position. He added a gre
his total in the second ha

Mayo: 2-8, Mea

*The ball was thrown
Grace, the Archbishop
Most Rev Dr Wa*

MAYO – S. Wynne, J.
Prendergast, S Flanaga
Staunton, H. Dixon, P. (
McAndrew, E. Mongey,
Carney, S. Mulder
Flanagan, T. Langan, J
Sub: L. Hastings for Dix

MEATH – K. Smyth, M.
O'Brien, K. McConnell (
(Capt), C. Kelly, C.
Connell, D. Taaffe, F.
McDonnell, P. Meegan,
J. O'Reilly, P. McDermo
Dixon for Hand, C. He
Heery.

BALLIN.
WELCOM
VICTORIO
MAYO TEA

BONFIRES, streamers an
greeted the Mayo team at
Tuesday night, on their fi
the town since winning

THE ALL-IRELAND CHAMPIONS – Front row (left to right) – Willie Casey (sub), Jackie Carney (trainer), Seán Wynne, Mick Flanagan, Eamonn Mongey, Seán Mulderrig, Rev. Peter Quinn, Padraig Carney, Seán Flanagan, Paddy Prendergast, Jimmy Curran, Joe Staunton. Back row (left to right): James Quinn, Eugene Quinn (brothers of Rev. Peter Quinn), Paddy Jordan (sub), Mick Loftus (sub), John Forde, Joe 'Joko' Gilvarry. Then Langan, Paddy Irwin, John McAndrew, Dr Jimmy Laffey (chairman of Mayo County Board), Henry Dixon, Liam Hastings (sub), Mick Mulderrig (sub), Gerald Courell (trainer), Pat Conway (treasurer, Mayo County Board).

GREAT DISPLAYS BY CARNEY, DIXON, QUINLAN & LANGAN

Western People

INCORPORATING THE "BALLINA HERALD"

THE LEADING JOURNAL OF THE PROVINCES.

VOL. 87.   Saturday, Nov. 30, 1963   Printed in Ireland   PRICE 5d

REVER A PIECE OF IRELAND ..

IN AMERICA THEY IM A HERO'S BURIAL

e golden days in Galway to days of black America. On Monday John Fitzgerald President of the United States, was ral procession through Washington to ional Cemetery amid scenes without the heads of sixty nations marched ow and family in a final tribute to the ee world.

mask of grief dignity in her lue Kennedy on control in her the admi- l. She walked n the White w's Cathedral weeping men hand her the n from many nt sympathy.

lera, his free dicating the of the man, t is the com- r for External ies.

roud day for ut the special i should have t of honour grave, proud ds in Irish t in final trib- tions of the to acknowl-

It was a bright cold day in the stunned city of Washington, a city crammed with moments and relic of the past, steeped in a sense of history and national prestige but now tragically aware of its new focus in the eyes of the world.

One of the most heart cutting moments of the entire ceremony came when Mrs Kennedy led her two children, Caroline and John- John, forward at the steps of the Cathedral to meet Cardinal Cushing. He placed a fatherly arm about her shoulders and spoke to the children as the TV cameras brought home yet another truth of the occasion – the loss of an ideal family man and husband to the private life overshadowed by the national loss.

Two million people crowded into Washington for the funeral and final tributes and almost a quarter of a million walked past the coffin as it lay in state under the great dome of the Capitol. A queue nine miles long at times sought to gain admission before

of a flame which will burn perpet- ually at Arlington by the widow of the murdered President. Then she turned to her last official duty won the hearts of the people of all — the reception of foreign digna- tories in the White House.

The courage of Jacqueline Kennedy all through from the

ative abroad. It would not be so had were it not for the fact that his memorable visit to Ireland won the hearts of the people of all classes and creeds.

Many people were so shocked by the tragic news that they can-

Mr O'Toole a large photograph of the President with his autograph "John F. Kennedy". On it are the words in the President's hand- writing, "Best wishes to Councillor O'Toole".

WESTPORT SOCCER

John F Kennedy as we remember him...

master of ceremonies.

CASTLEBAR
In Castlebar people were shocked at the news of the President's assassination. The tri- colour on the Courthouse flew at half-mast, and everywhere there was a general air of mourning, as townspeople followed the dra- matic events through newspapers, television and radio.

Following consultation between Mr. Michael Neary, chairman of Castlebar Urban Council, the town clerk and several councill- ors, it was decided to send a telegram of sympathy to the American Embassy on Monday.

Justice Hugh McGahon adjourned a special court in Castlebar on Monday evening for fifteen minutes while the President's funeral was taking place.

At all Masses in the Church of Our Lady of the Holy Rosary, Castlebar, on Sunday, the prayers of the faithful were asked for the repose of Mr Kennedy's soul.

CLAREMORRIS
Requiem Mass was offered in Claremorris on Tuesday morning by Rev Thomas Concannon, C.C., for the repose of the soul of the late President. All business houses, local banks, and the local Vocational School were closed during the Mass. The pupils and teachers of the Vocational School marched in procession to the Church.

Asking prayers for the deceased, the clergy urged the congregation to pray that God will give spiritual strength to Mrs. Kennedy, and the members of the Kennedy family, to carry their heavy cross with faith and resig- nation, and to speed the day when the ideals for which the President

Council, despatched condolence to the w American Emba Park, Dublin, cons found sympathy of t ple and that of the Council who rep Only last June Mr i the privilege of each ings with the dead function at the t Dublin.

BALLINA
Large number Solemn Requiem Muredach's Cathed Tuesday morning at the late Preside Business premise establishments clo their staffs to atte the celebrant of wl Rev G. Moore, Adn J Harte, C.C.; rober Tuffy, C.C., and m monies, Very Rev President, St Mures Clergy from S College attended.

Schools in the closed and flags fle from public and pri

Large crowds a which was celeb Cathedral for the on Monday mornin Tribute was pai President Kennedy Service in the Met in Ballina, and offered on beh Kennedy and famil

In the Presby prayers were als behalf of the berea

KILLALA
In Killala Cathed Rev Rev Bu preached the sermo President Kenned

THE BUFFALO OF CONNEMARA

CONNEMARA is a region in the West of Ireland where luminous white waves burst and spray upward from great dark fingers of jutting rock, a place where my friends speak Gaelic. Its the place where I first had the thought and feeling for a painting like this.

A few days earlier I had been in Manhattan's Battery Park, the point of entry for generations of Irish. My friend Don Mullan and I had just visited the National Museum of the American Indian across the street. The late afternoon, the museum visit, the empty park, and the Statue of Liberty in the harbor all came together to evoke the memory of a quote from something I read;

"They are going! They are going! The Irish are going with a vengeance! Soon a Celt will be as rare on the banks of the Liffey as a Red Man on the shores of Manhattan".
                                        The London Times 1847

Black 47, the height of Ireland's Great Famine had also been the year that my people, the Choctaw, collected from "meager resources" the sum of $170 for Irish Famine victims, shortly after our own epic Trail of Tears. The donation was reported by another paper of the day, The Arkansas Intelligencer as "the poor Indian sending his mite to the poor Irish".

Standing on the Connemara shoreline, I thought of how remarkable it was that two poor, dispossessed, and separate nations had been connected by a singular moment of sharing. It also occurred to me that the old 1847 staff of The London Times would probably be as stunned to know that both the Irish and the American Indian have survived, as they would be to see a buffalo hunt on the shores of Connemara.

THE BUFFALO OF CONNEMARA is a somewhat whimsical celebration of the survival of the Irish and Choctaw as separate but connected peoples. As dawn breaks over Ireland, buffalo thunder across the Connemara surf. To Native America, the buffalo is a symbol of prosperity and thanksgiving.

THE BUFFALO OF CONNEMARA was completed in Ireland during my residency in Co. Clare, and was exhibited at the American Embassy in Dublin at the invitation of US Ambassador Jean Kennedy-Smith. Additional exhibitions included Derry City, Carrickfergus, the Bank of Ireland's Art Centre, and The Late Late show, Ireland's longest running television program.

THE BUFFALO OF CONNEMARA signature print was published in Ireland, and first released in America at the Boston Irish Festival.

For more information please contact: PO Box 5244
                                          Dublin 12
                                          Ireland

In the mid nineteen fifties, Cwm Tryweryn including the village of Capel Celyn in North Wales was drowned to guarantee the water supply for the city of Liverpool. The entire community ceased to exist with the drowning of farms, post office, school, church, graveyard.

Éamonn de Valera sent the following message of support to the group fighting for the existence of the community.

When against terrific odds a small nation is seeking to preserve its personality and culture the destruction of any area where the language and national characteristics have been traditionally preserved would be a misfortune which every effort should be made to avoid.

Material economic advantages are far too dearly bought when secured at the loss of an inspiring spiritual inheritance and some modern efficiency enthusiasts need to have this fact forcibly impressed upon them.

When alternatives which do not involve such a loss are available, all who believe that man has needs other than those of the body will sympathise with the people of the Welsh nation in their efforts to see that alternatives to the Tryweryn scheme be found and adopted. I wish you every success.

Éamon de Valéra

Sept. 24, 1956.   Dail Eireann, Dublin.

Irish NATIONAL ANTHEM

Irish NATIONAL ANTHEM

A Soldier's Song

Soldiers are we,
whose Lives are pledged to Ireland
Some have come from a Land Beyond the wave
Sworn to be free,
no more our Ancient sireland
Shall shelter the despot or the slave:
Tonight we man the Bearna Baoghil
In Erin's cause,
come woe or weal;
Mid cannon's roar and rifle's peal
We'll chant a soldier's song.

Amhrán Na bhFiann

Sinne Fianna Fáil
atá fá gheall ag Éirinn,
buidhean dár sluagh tar tuinn do ráinig
chughainn:
Faobhar bheith saor,
sean-tír ár sinnsear feasta
Ní fágear fá'n tíorán ná fá'n tráil;
Anocht a theigeamh sa Bhearna Baoghil,
Le gean ar Ghaedhil chun báis nó saoghail,
Le gunna sgréac fá Lámhach na bpiléar,
Seo Libh, canaidh Amhrán na bhFiann.

We'll sing a song, a soldier's song
With cheering, rousing chorus
As round our blazing fires we throng,
The starry heavens o'er us;
Impatient for the coming fight,
And as we wait the mornings light
Here in the silence of the night
We'll sing a soldier's song

CHORUS

In valley green or towering crag
Our fathers fought before us,
And conquered 'neath the same old flag
That's proudly floating o'er us,
We're children of a fighting race
That never yet has known disgrace,
And as we march the foe to face,
We'll sing a soldier's song

CHORUS

Sons of the Gael ! Men of the Pale !
The long watched day is breaking;
The serried ranks of Innisfail
Shall set the tyrant quaking.
Our camp fires now are burning low;
See in the east a silvery glow,
Out yonder waits the Saxon foe,
So sing a soldier's song.

Seo dhíbh a cháirde duan oglaigh
Caithréimeach, bríoghmhar, ceolmhar,
Ár dteinte cnámh go buacach táid,
'S an spéir go mín réaltógach.
Is fionmhar faobhrach sinn chum gleo
'S go tiúnmhar glé roimh tigheacht do'n ló,
Fa ciúnas chaoimh na h-oidhche ar seol,
Seo libh, canaidh Amhrán na bhFiann.

CURFA

Cois banta réidhe, ar árdaibh sléibhe
Ba bhuadhach ár sinnsear romhainn,
Ag lámhach go tréan fá'n sár-bhrat séin
Tá thuas sa ghaoith go seolta:
Ba dhuthchas riamh d'ár gcine cháidh
Gan iompáil siar ó i.nirt áir,
'Siubhal mar iad i gcoinnibh námhaid
Seo libh, canaidh Amhrán na bhFiann.

CURFA

A buidhean nach fann d'fuil Ghaoidheal is Gall,
Sinn breacadh lae na saoirse,
Tá sgéimhle 's sgannradh i gcroidhthibh namhad,
Roimh ranngaibh laochra ár dtíre;
Ár dteinte is tréith gan spréach anois,
Sin luisne ghlé san spéir anoir,
'S an bíodhbha i raon na bpiléar agaibh:
Seo libh, can aidh Amhrán na bhFiann.

The Battle of the Boreen

One of the most memorable happenings here was the 'Battle of the Boreen' which happened in October 1881. The years 1879 and 1880 were famine years, so by 1881 people had fallen into arrears with their rent. The sheriff and police were on the road every day exicting families who could not meet the rent by Gale day. They were ruthless. A woman partially naked was thrown out of her poor cabin in Pullathomas. Peter O'Malley of Glencastle, the rates collector, had made several efforts to collect rates in this townland without success. The local people here knew that the next move would be the serving of a summons on all the defaulters by Richard Barrett, also of Glencastle who was the process server. A meeting of the Land League was held to discuss matters. At the meeting it was decided to mobilise the locals so as to prevent either Barrett or O'Malley from entering the village. Barrett sought police protection and on October 27th 1881, with forty-three police drawn from Belmullet, Rossport, Glenamoy, Clencalry and Bangor, he set out for Graughill with a batch of summonses.

By the time they reached Graughill about one hundred people had assembled at a low lying boreen leading to the village. Sub-Inspector Matthew Stritch, from Belmullet, leading the police force, issued a warning to the people and then marched the police protecting Barrett into the boreen towards the village. A battle ensued, Ellen McDonagh, aged 23, was fatally stabbed, Mary Deane, was seriously wonded. They had come to evict Mary Deane and her family from her house. A five year old child ran outside and Mary ran after her. Mary Deane was shot; she died nine days later of gunshot wounds. A large number of civilians were wounded. Twenty people were taken prisoner and lodged in Castlebar jail. An inquest on the deaths of Ellen McDonagh and Mary Deane was held in Belmullet before Mr. W.C. Moroney Resident Magistrate, Robert Mostyn was Coroner; George Bolton Crown Solicitor, representing the police and C. McInerney, Barrister, respresenting the injured person. Doctor Mullen of Bangor, who had carried out a post mortem examination of the bodies, declared that Ellen McDonagh was bayoneted and Mary Deane died as a result of gunshot wounds to the throat.

At this inquest the Catholic clery of the locality requested that the prisoners should be released on bail so as to attend. Mr Moroney R.M. permitted the release of the prisoners on £20 bail each, paid by the clergy.

There had been some reluctance on the part of the police to procure a jury for the next inquest. Mr Carter, landlord and his friend Mr Crampton, both Justices Of The Peace, were fined for declining to attend. Eventually sixteen men of the Erris district were sworn as a jury. Mr. McNulty, manager of the Hibernian Bank, Belmullet, was foreman of the jury. The jury was taken to the scene of the affray at Graughill and the bodies exhumed for their inspection as was the custom.

At the inquest Belmullet was thronged and the court crowded. All the shops were closed. James Mills of Gortmellia, "a young man of much intelligence" stated that on the 27th October 1881, he was standing on the verge of the boreen leading from the village to the main road when he saw forty police led by Sub-Inspector Stritch approaching. The local people were in the fields on both sides of the boreen. Constable McDonald of Rossport pulled a lad, Anthony Deane over one of the fences on the boreen and "placed the boy between himself and another policeman using him cruelly enough. The boy's brother rushed to his rescue and the police used him cruelly also. Then a third brother rushed out and was also arrested and cruelly treated."

Sub-Inspector Stritch gave the oder to fix bayonets and directly afterwards shouted charge. The police jumped over the boreen fence into the field where they bayoneted every man, woman and child that came in their way. About one hundred persons with present. They fled as fast as they could and the police pursued bayoneting any person they caught. The police stopped after about 150 yards and I heard the officer giving the order to fire. Some people fled, others continued running and some hid behind houses and stacks of hay and corn.

Anthony Monagthan of Inver stated that the arrest of the boy was the cause of the affray. "I did not see any stones thrown until the police bagan to fire."

Pat Keenaghan said, "The police had a frightful appearance. They appeared drunk. One policeman jumped into the field and stabbed James Mills on the right hip. I saw no stones thrownbefore the police charged."

Ned Munnelly (an Irish witness) said he was arrested by a drunken policeman who had lost a bottle of poteen which was produced in Court.

Richard Barrett (Summons server) stated that when he and the police came to the boreen, things were quiet until the people were arrested. He did not see any policeman injured nor did he see any stones thrown before the police charged.

John Egan, a policeman from Belmullet stated, "a little boy named Deane standing on a ditch with the crowd, threw a stone and was arrested. Some people jumped into the boreen to rescue the boy. The officer gave the order to fix bayonetrs and push back the people. The police got into the field and drove the people back. The people then turned and threw stones at the police. The order to fire was then given by Sub-Inspectore Matthew Stritch."

Under cross examination, he said he did not see any polivemen struck with a stone.

Terence Reilly, another policeman said, "I carried on that day, forty rounds of ammunition, twelve buckshot, and twenty eight balls." When asked if he killed any person, he replied, "I cannot say."

John Kilker, a policeman from Bangor said, "The arrest of Anthony Deane was the beginning of the row."

Darby Mills of Gortmellia said that it was Constable Sullivan of Rossport who shot Mary Deane.

Sub-Inspectore Matthew Stritch when cross examined, said he did not know of any of his men being struck by stones before he gave the order to charge or fire. "The locals seemed to be uncommonly plucky people," he stated.

After two hour recession of December 5th 1881, the jury found Constable John Sullivan and Sub-Inspector Stritch guilty of wilful murder.

Mr. McInerney requested that warrants be issued immediately for the arrest of both Sullivan and Stritch.

Mr. Bolton, on behalf of the police said, "if the warrants are issued, I caution any officer who gets then for execution, not to act upon them, and I warn them not to dare imprison these men, even for a single moment."

The Coroner said, "I intend to issue my warrants tomorrow."

Warrants were issued and the case known as *"The Queen v Stritch"* was fixed for hearing on April 29th 1882.
Mr W.C. Moroney, Resident Magistrate, who always showed a special sympathy towards the poor of Erris wrote to Dublin Castle,

asking to be excluded, and stated; "As resident Magistrate of the district I have been a good deal mixed up with the Graughill affair, therefore, I have a great objective to taking part in the inquiry which is about to take place… I shall feel much obliged if the Attorney General would relieve my of any partipation in the proceedings.

Matthew Stritch, aged 34, a native of Roscommon and John Sullivan were charged and brought to trial. They were eventually freed on grounds of self defence. The expenses in connection with the prosecution of Sub-Inspector Stritch was £39.10.0 and was paid by the state.

In March of 1882 the Graughill prisoners were brought to trial in Castlebar Courthouse. They were indicted on charges of riot and unlawful assembly. The hearing lasted three days. On the third day they were discharged from custody and walked home to Erris.

A song was composed called, "The Battle of the Boreen"

O Brethren dear did you hear
What happened here below?
In the barony of Erris
Near Inver in Mayo.

The recorded feats of other years
Are nothing when compared
To the trials and tribulations
That our native here have shared.

Mary Deane died as result of a gunshot wounds she received during the battle of the boreen. The battle took place on 27th October 1881. She and her family were being evicted from her house. A five year old child ran out of the house and Mary ran out after her and she was shot. She died nine days later.

Danny Deane, a nephew of Mary, resided on the land years later and he married Mary McGuire. Danny Deanes' brother left Graughill for America when he was sixteen years old. There he joined the army and ascended through the ranks to Colonel. He was a highly decorated officer. He gained recognition in the Irish media due to his highly regarded reputation in the army.

Collection of Poems, Promises & Prayers

I used to sell fish here in Doooma, door to door,
I delivered the fish to the customer, to house.
It was a very bad winter, wind and rain.
And the people bring me in and make some food
for me and tea.
And then years later, I was very young then,
I met a girl at a dance who was living next
door to the post office and we became friends
and we were dancing and she was one of the
first girlfriend I danced with.
She left home and went ot England and she
told me we would meet up three months later
and we never mer up again.
When eventually we met again we were both
married and had kids.
And we talked about our dancing time and both
our lives and we bacame friends.
Years later I met her at her father's funeral
and we chatted and talked.
There was a reason we had to meet again and
it all made sense. She shared her problems in
life and I was able to help her to move on to a
better way in life.

Patrick Flannery from
Flannery village near Barnatra

To my Dearest Family

Some things we would like to say, but first of all to let you know we all arrived okay. We are writing this from heaven where we dwell with God above, where there's no more tears or sadness, there is just eternal love.

Please do not be unhappy just because we're out of sight remember that we're with you every morning, noon and night.

That day we had to leave you, when our time on earth was through, God picked us up and hugged us and he said I welcome you. It's good to have you back again, you were missed while you were gone, as for your dearest family they'll be here later on. I need you here so badly as part of my big plan, there's so much that we have to do to help our mortal man.

Then God gave us a list of things, He wished for us to do and foremost on that list of ours is to watch and care for you. And we will be beside you every day, week and year and when you're sad we're standing there to wipe away your tears.

And when you lie in bed at night, the day's chores put to flight, God and we're closest to you in the middle of the night.

When you think of our life on Earth and all those loving years because you are only human they are bound to bring you tears. But do not be afraid to cry, it does relieve the pain, remember there would be no flowers unless there was some rain.

We wish that we could tell you of all that God has planned, but if we were to tell you wouldn't understand
But one thing is for certain though our life on Earth is ore we're closer to you now than we ever were before.

And to our very many friends trust God knows best.
We're still not far away from you, we're just beyond the crest.

There are rocky roads ahead of you and many hills to climb but together we can do it taking one day at a time. It was always our philosophy and we'd like it for you too, that as you give unto the world so the world will give to you.

THE TWELVE TRADITIONS OF ALCOHOLICS ANONYMOUS

1. Our common welfare should come first; personal recovery depends upon A.A. unity.

2. For our group purpose there is but one ultimate authority – a loving God as He may express Himself in our group conscience. Our leaders are but trusted servants; they do not govern.

3. The only requirement for A.A. membership is a desire to stop drinking.

4. Each group should be autonomous except in matters affecting other groups or A.A. as a whole.

5. Each group has but one primary purpose – to carry its message to the alcoholic who still suffers.

6. An A.A. group ought never endorse, finance, or lend the A.A. name to any related facility or outside enterprise, lest problems of money, property, and prestige divert us from our primary purpose.

7. Every A.A. group ought to be fully self-supporting, declining outside contributions.

8. Alcoholics Anonymous should remain forever nonprofessional, but our service centers may employ special workers.

9. A.A., as such, ought never be organized; but we may create service boards or committees directly responsible to those they serve.

10. Alcoholics Anonymous has no opinion on outside issues; hence the A.A. name ought never be drawn into public controversy.

11. Our public relations policy is based on attraction rather than promotion; we need always maintain personal anonymity at the level of press, radio and films.

12. Anonymity is the spiritual foundation of all our Traditions, ever reminding us to place principles before personalities.

Reprinted with permission – Alcoholics Anonymous World Services

Why We Drank

We drank for happiness and became unhappy

We drank for joy and became miserable

We drank for sociability and became argumentative

We drank for sophistication and became obnoxious

We drank for friendship and we made enemies

We drank for sleep and awakened without rest

We drank for strength and felt weak

We drank medicinally and acquired health problems

We drank for relaxation and got the shakes

We drank for bravery and became afraid

We drank for confidence and became doubtful

We drank to make conversation easier and slurred our speech

We drank to forget and were forever haunted

We drank to feel heavenly and ended up feeling like hell

We drank for freedom and became slaves

We drank to erase our problems and saw them multiply

We drank to cope with life and invited death

DESIDERATA

GO PLACIDLY amid the noise and the haste, and remember what peace there may be in silence. As far as possible, without surrender, be on good terms with all persons. Speak your truth quietly and clearly; and listen to others, even to the dull and the ignorant; they too have their story. Avoid loud and aggressive persons; they are vexatious to the spirit. If you compare yourself with others, you may become vain or bitter, for always there will be greater and lesser persons than yourself. Enjoy your achievements as well as your plans. Keep interested in your own career, however humble; it is a real possession in the changing fortunes of time. Exercise caution in your business affairs, for the world is full of trickery. But let this not blind you to what virtue there is; many persons strive for high ideals, and everywhere life is full of heroism. Be yourself. Especially, do not feign affection. Neither be cynical about love; for in the face of all aridity and disenchantment it is as perennial as the grass. Take kindly the counsel of the years, gracefully surrendering the things of youth. Nurture strength of spirit to shield you in sudden misfortune. But do not distress yourself with dark imaginings. Many fears are born of fatigue and loneliness. Beyond a wholesome discipline, be gentle with yourself. You are a child of the universe no less than the trees and the stars; you have a right to be here. And whether or not it is clear to you, no doubt the universe is unfolding as it should. Therefore be at peace with God, whatever you conceive Him to be. And whatever your labors and aspirations, in the noisy confusion of life, keep peace in your soul. With all its sham, drudgery and broken dreams, it is still a beautiful world. Be cheerful. Strive to be happy. *Max Ehrmann*

Prayer to the Holy Spirit

You made me see everything, and showed me the way to reach my goal. You who give me the divine gift to forgive and forget the wrong that is done to me, and you who are with me in all instances of my life. I thank you for everything and confirm once more that I never want to be separated from you, no matter how great the material desires may be. I want to be with my love ones in your perpetual glory.

Thank you for your love towards me and my love ones. Amen.

Say this for three consective days, ask no favours favours will be granted after the third day. Publicaion as promised.

Novena to St Jude

May the Sacred Heart of Jesus be adored, glorified, loved and preserved, throughout the world, now and forever. Sacred Heart of Jesus, pray for us. St. Jude worker of miracles, pray for us. St Jude, helper of the helpless, pray for us. Amen.

I suggest that you say this prayer for 9 days, 9 times a day, and by the eighth da, you will have an answer. (If it's God's will) Never known to fail.

P.S. Say 10 Hail Mary's every Tuesday to St Anne, Tuesdays are St Anne's Day for favours. Her Special Day.

Prayer to the Blessed Virgin (Never known to fail)

Oh most beautiful flower of Mount Carmel, Fruitful Vine, splender of Heaven, Blessed mother of the Son of God, Immaculate Virgin, assist me in this my necessity, there are none who can withstand your power. Oh star of the sea, help me and show me you are my mother. Oh Mary conceived without sin, pray for us who have recourse to thee. (Three times) Holy Mary I place this cause in your hands. (Three Times)

This prayer must be said for three says and after thress days the request will be granted. (Will never fail) a copy of this prayer must be published immediately or given to a friend.

Jesus said:

"Do not be afraid, I am with you."

Miracle Prayer

Message of Hope and Healing
Thank you Jesus
For your Miracle of
Saving us during the heavy rainfall
and turf slide on Friday evening
19th September 2003.
In the near future
A sign will come from Heaven
to correct the conscience
of the world followed by
A Great Miracle
Performed by our Saviour Jesus
The following Spring
or early Summer
on a Thursday evening
around half past eight.

Eigeem Eome
Baile Eone
Glengad + Cilcommon + Erris

O, Great Spirit
Whose voice I hear in the winds,
And whose breath gives life to all the world,
hear me. I am small and weak. I need your
strength and wisdom.

Let me walk in beauty, and make my eyes
ever behold the red and purple sunset.

Make my hands respect the things I have
made and my ears sharp to hear your voice.

Make me wise so that I may understand the
things you have taught my people.

Let me learn the lessons you have hidden
in every leaf and rock.

I seek strength, not to be greater than my
brother, but to fight my greatest
enemy - myself.

Make me always ready to come to you with
clean hands and straight eyes.

So when life fades, as the fading sunset,
my spirit may come to you without shame.

A Sioux Indian Prayer

During the time of the Famine in Ireland, all the American Indian Tribes raised 10,000 dollars to send to Irish families.
The English Government that brought the famine to Ireland & the Queen of England at the time, give 5 pounds.
We should be always grateful for the American Indian Tribes for what they did for the Irish during the Famine years and remember all the pain that they suffered during times of war.

If you can help somebody who's in sorrow or in pain, then you can say to God at night my day was not in vain. And now we are contented that our life it was worthwhile knowing as we passed along the way we made somebody smile.

So if you meet somebody who is down and feeling low, just lend a hand to pick him up as on your way you go

When you are walking down the steet and you've got us on your mind, we're walking in your footsteps, only half a step behind.

And when you feel the gentle breeze or the wind upon your face, that's us giving you a great big hug or just a soft embrace.

And when it's time for you to go from that body to be free, remember you're not going, you're coming home to us.

And we will always love you from that land way up above. Will be in touch again soon.

P.S. God sends his Love.